The Death of the Siamese Twins & Other Plays

by

Louis Phillips

ISBN 978-1-934209-30-1

10-digit ISBN 1-934209-30-9

$16.99

303 Park Avenue South, #1440

New York, NY 10010-3657

Cover design by M. Stefan Strozier (www.mstefanstrozier.org)

World Audience (www.worldaudience.org) is a global consortium of artists and writers, producing the literary journal *audience* and *The audience Review.*. Our periodicals and books are edited by M. Stefan Strozier and assistant editors. Please submit your stories, poems, paintings, photography or other artwork to submissions@worldaudience.org. Inquire about being a reviewer: theatre@worldaudience.org. Thank you.

The Death of the Siamese Twins & Other Plays

by

Louis Phillips

A World Audience Book

(www.worldaudience.org)

May, 2007

New York

Dedicated to Robert Karmon,

fellow playwright & partner-in-crime.

TABLE OF CONTENTS

THE DEATH OF THE SIAMESE TWINS

A play in one-act by Louis Phillips

Lulu, the Siamese twins. At far stage left there is a half-opened window with a thermometer dangling from a short brown cord. On the sill is a little photometer that turns and turns with the rays of the sun.

HOSS: Flag's up, sisters.
VOICE: (*from behind the door*) Hold your horses, will ya?
HOSS: Can't find anything out here. Who put the milk in the garbage last night? It was a full quart of milk ...Mary H., Joseph, and Jesus, if the Governor ran the Crumb Castle the way you run this apartment of yours, he'd be out of business before you could say Joe Blow.
VOICE: (*from behind the door*) Button up, Banana Nose. You got your dukie, didn't you?
HOSS: Hurry up, you two. Joe Blow's almost ready.

Sound of toilet flushing.

VOICE: (*from behind the door*) We're coming, we're coming...
HOSS: Mary H., Joseph, and Jesus, you two have been in the donniker all morning. You'd think somebody else might like to get in there.

The door opens and there are Lena and Lulu. Dressed in identical pink dresses with slits cut in the side to accommodate the small band of flesh that joins them at the waist, they stand side by side in the doorway glaring at Hoss. With the exception of the extreme inconvenience of being joined together for life, the two women are striking and energetic. They're in their late twenties or early thirties, but they look a bit older. Lulu has a small scar on her forehead, but it's not at all noticeable when she covers it with her hair. Lena appears to be the slightly better groomed of the two, and she's a bit more phlegmatic than her sister. Like Hoss, they too have seen their share of carnivals, small circuses, and assorted fairs. Lulu wears a locket and a ring; Lena wears no Jewelry at all.

LULU: Like who?
HOSS: Like me, that's who.

LULU: For a moment, I thought you were inviting more of your Lot Lice up.

They move from the doorway.

LULU: So, use it. Who's stopping you?

Hoss enters and shuts the door.

LULU: You know what this is? This is just a grab joint to him ...*(to* Hoss)...You wobble in here on some Saturday, after we ain't seen you for five or six years, you get yourself a couple of free meals, grab a little ass, and then you're off again, chasing any rundown glorified Lint that'll take you on.
LENA: Don't start anything, willya, Lulu?

Lulu and Lena walk toward center stage, and Lulu removes a white silk handkerchief from the pocket of her dress. She daubs her face with it

LULU: This is going to be a good juice day. I can feel it already...what's the temperature say?
LENA: I can't read it from here.
LULU: Let me look.
LENA: We have to watch the pancake.
LULU: (*trying to turn toward the thermometer*) Why? Is it going anywhere?... It'll only take a second. How long does it take to read a thermometer? It's not as if it's a book or something.
LENA: Let's set the table. The gorilla never sets the table.
LULU: I'm not moving unless we see how hot it is ...It feels like we're Down Yonder.
LENA: You'll move or I'll kick your shin in...
LULU: And you know what'll happen to you...
LENA: I don't understand you, Lulu, ever since Hoss shows up here, you've been acting like a two-bit First of May...I'm getting a bit fed up...
LULU: We don't need anyone of that Lot Lice up here ...Every time one of those gorillas gets a bit thin, they're up here mooching off Lena and Lulu, the Charity Sisters of Sigma Chi... Anything that has got a mouth...
LENA: The pancake's burning,

LULU: No.
LENA: You'll move or I'll tell Charlie not to give you any breakfast...You talking about mouth...that's a hot one...

Lulu kicks Lena in the shins. Lena tries to step on Lulu's bare foot. Lulu, who has the right arm, grabs Lena's hair. Lena, who has the left arm, grabs Lulu's hair. Hoss comes out of the bathroom buckling his pants.

HOSS: Now what in hell is going on? Mary H., Joseph, and Jesus, stop it. (He grabs their arms and stops the tangle) Isn't it too hot to be carrying on like this?...
LULU: How do I know how hot it is? I don't get to see the thermometer.
HOSS: And look at the pancake.
LENA: It's Lulu's fault.
HOSS: Mary H., Joseph, and Jesus ...it's blacker than ...sit down ...both of you...
LULU: Well, only one of us sure ain't gonna sit down.

Hoss crosses to the window and looks angrily at the thermometer.

HOSS: It's already in the eighties and it's not even ten o'clock yet...

Lulu and Lena sit on the bench facing the audience.

LENA: On days like this, you have to get up early if you want to get any work done.
LULU: No getting up in a tunnel for this girl.

Hoss opens the cupboard over the sink, removes some plates and cups. He quickly sets the table for breakfast.

HOSS: Temperature's what you feel.
LULU: I feel lousy.
HOSS: When I'm working, I don't feel it. Sometimes we'd be Down Yonder and it would be over a hundred degrees in the shade, but if I were working under the rag, I would hardly feel it...
LULU: He's under the rag and I'm on it...some combination.

LENA: Charlie, let me ask your opinion on something. Lulu's got this brainstorm that we should study meteorology and get a television show somewhere ...She thinks we could be weather forecasters.
LULU: Lena'll take the East coast and I'll take the West...The public loves gimmicks like that.
LENA: What do you think Charlie? I think it's tough for women to break into that field.
HOSS: What do either of you know about weather?
LULU: What does anybody know about weather, for Chrissakes? They make it up the way everything else is made up.
HOSS: Tying a thermometer on a string doesn't make you an expert.
LULU: Stow it, willya? I can predict weather as well as any of those gorillas. You just get up in front of a map, and you say hot front, cold front, *tornadoes* in Meenasota...How tough is that?
HOSS: It's not *Meenasota.*
LULU: It is to me.
HOSS: You know what I think?
LULU: You think the moon is made out of green cheese ...That's what you think.
HOSS: I think you should stick to what you know ...People are happier among their own kind.
LENA: Listen to Charlie, Lulu.
LULU: Our own kind, huh? That should narrow the field considerably. How many other Siamese Twins do you know wandering around here? And you want us to stick to our own kind.
LENA: That's not what he means, Lulu, and you know it.
HOSS: If you go anywhere near television, they'll use you for a test pattern...That's what they'll use you for.
LULU: Oh, get him!
LENA: No pancakes for me, Charlie ...I'm on a diet.
LULU: With his cooking he'll put everybody on a diet.
HOSS: That was the one you were supposed to watch.
LULU: They let Hoss work the Crumb Castle one season and Tina the Fat Lady dropped four hundred pounds ... She's been out of work ever since.

Charlie places some pancakes on Lulu's plate. Lena rummages through the plastic fruit and finds a real pear.

HOSS: Try these and maybe you won't work your mouth so much.
LULU: (*to Hoss*) Hand me the Flookum there...and the club soda ...wouldja? Thanks.

Lulu mixes the powder and soda water and makes herself a soft drink to *wash down Hoss's pancakes.*

LENA: I don't see how she drinks that crap for breakfast..must be rotting her stomach out...
LULU: Keep track of your own stomach ...I'm not the one who keeps us in the donniker all morning...we'd be in and out in the shake of a flea's tail...
HOSS: *(sits down)* Fleas don't have tails.
LULU: Well, if they don't, it's the only tail you've missed.
LENA: Don't mind her, Charlie. It's just that time of the month.
LULU: I wish men would get cramps. Then maybe they would understand things once in a while.
LENA: Can you get me an onion, Charlie?
LULU: Oh no you don't...
LENA: I can have an onion with my pear if l want to...
LULU: Not if I have to smell your stinking breath all day...
LENA: You can look the other way...
LULU: All day?

Hoss gets up, goes to the half-refrigerator and brings Lena a large red onion.

LULU: Some people just have no consideration.
LENA: I have more consideration than you.
LULU: Why don't you go to the store, Hoss, and see if Kellog's don't put out onion and radish cereal ..Then you two would have it knocked in the shade.
HOSS: Lena, honey, maybe you ought to eat something else for breakfast..
LULU: I don't see how she has the nerve to kick about my *Flookum,* when she eats that stuff...

Lena takes a big bite out of the raw onion.

LENA: What I eat is healthy for you.
LULU: Healthy for you, maybe. It don't do a thing for me.
LENA: Remember what mama said about carrying an onion in your pocket to ward off disease...Look how many mud shows we've been with and never caught a cold yet.
HOSS: Your momma should have told you that you wouldn't get kissed either.
LULU: You should have thought of that last night.

Lena picks up the remains of the broken balloon.

LENA: What's this Larry here? Is this my giraffe?...There's Lulu's dog ...Where's my giraffe?
HOSS: Give me the fink...I'll throw it away...
LENA: But what did you do to it?...
HOSS: I didn't do anything to it. Things bust, that's all...Don't worry, I'll make you another one.
LENA: But I like the one you made last night.
LULU: Let him make another one...Banana Nose needs the practice...He needs to practice on a lot of things...

Hoss tosses the balloon pieces into the garbage bin.

HOSS: Hey, that's hitting a little low, Lulu...
LULU: I was talking about your cooking. I don't know what you think I was talking about.
HOSS: I don't think you like me.
LULU: Momma always told me that three in a bed is unlucky.
HOSS: I can take a hint.

Lena kicks Lulu in the ankle

LULU: Cut it out, Lena.

Lena blows some of her onion-breath in Lulu's face.

LENA: Ever since that jig High-boy upped and left you, you've been jealous of anything with pants that come around here...

LULU: Take the Brown Cow, willya? I've got nothing against Banana Nose, but this ain't the Waldorf Astoria. The landlady won't even let us keep a cat...How's she going to feel about this gorilla?
HOSS: It's not as if we need a mender. I've only been here three days. That isn't a lifetime...
LULU: Three days with some men is a lifetime.
HOSS: Give me a break. You know the Governor needs a rubber man and punk pusher ...I'm going down there as soon as we're done eating and I'm going to see if he won't take me on...Then I'll be out of your hair. If that's what you want...
LULU: It's not my hair you've been in.
LENA: See, I told you she's jealous...
HOSS: I don't know why your mother just didn't saw you apart in the first place. It's a simple enough operation. One of you at a time is enough...
LENA: Momma thought it would be unlucky to split us...God's will and all that, you know...
LULU: God's some kidder, all righL.In that great Paper Section in the sky, the suckers with halos are just waiting for Lulu and Lena, the Siamese angels, to gawk at...
HOSS: You're old enough now...
LULU: The trauma would kill us...
LENA: Charlie, we were born face to face, and each day momma would get down on her knees to pray, and each day she would stretch us just a little bit more apart .Each day the band of flesh that holds us together would become more and more elastic until we were able to stand side by side...
LULU: Not far enough to suit me especially when you two are playing Romeo and Juliet...
LENA: I didn't mind when you were making it with the High-boy...
LULU: That was different. He wasn't Lot Lice coming up here to mooch off us...
HOSS: Look, I'll square the beef if you want. How much do I owe you?
LENA: Don't listen to her, Charlie ...We ain't taking money for you.
LULU: What difference does it make if we wanted to or not? He hasn't got any coconuts in his grouch bag.
HOSS: I'm getting some... as soon as I sign...
LULU: Before the season's over, you'll be sleeping in corn fiakes.

HOSS: *(Loudly changing the subject)* You want some Java?
LULU: Invite the neighbors in while you're at it.
HOSS: When you've spieled as much as I have, you forget how loud you really are.
LULU: It's nothing to threesheet about.
HOSS: Mary H., Joseph, and Jesus, should I heat the pot or not?
LULU: Why not?
LENA: When is Mother's Day? I think we missed momma's day this year.
LULU: Some momma. She would have put us in a notchhouse if it were up to her, turning tricks for every Chang and Eng who came along ...Stand up...
LENA: What for?
LULU: I want to put my pup-tents on ...I'm tired of going barefoot.
LENA: Not until I finish breakfast.
LULU: How long can it take to eat an onion?
LENA: I want some mud to wash it down with.
LULU: You're going to do what I tell you...

Hoss puts the water on the stove for coffee, then turns to keep the peace.

HOSS: I'm going to have to meet your momma someday.
LULU: What for? You want her ass, too?
LENA: We send her a card once a year ...used to...
LULU: Took every coconut we had...
HOSS: You must have put some away for a rainy day...
LULU: Nope...Even queer ducks need a pond to paddle in...
LENA: She has a grease joint in Minnesota.
LULU: Used to.
HOSS: Then you're thin, too...
LULU: Try invisible ...If you're interested in Lena for her coconuts, forget it. You'd be better off shacking up with our landlady.
LENA: Oh, Lulu, give yourself the brown cow, will ya?
LULU: Not until you get up and we go get my pup-tents and you brush your teeth...

Lena glares at her sister, slams the onion on the table. The sisters get up, cross in to the donniker, where we can see them standing over the twin sinks brushing their teeth...

HOSS: I'm not interested in Lena for her imaginary coconuts...
LULU: What do I know? I'm only the left half of this dynamic duo...

Hoss takes some balloons from the box and blows one up quickly. Perhaps he'll twist it into an apple or an animal.

HOSS: I suppose you get marriage offers every day of the week.

Lena and Lulu return to the common room and walk over to the bed, where Lulu slips into a pair of red overshoes.

LULU: That shows how much you know.
HOSS: I don't know.
LULU: We're novelty items. Everybody loves novelty items.

Hoss crosses to the stove, pours the boiling water into cups to make coffee. Lulu picks up a gold locket from the night stand and opens it.

LENA: Lulu had a High-boy sweet on her once...
LULU: *(Opening the locket)* I'm not talking about him...I'm talking about him.
HOSS: *(Looking toward the locket)* Who's he?
LULU: Just some John Law from South Carolina...
LENA: How can you talk about Earl that way?
LULU: You're right, kid...Earl was a sweet kid.
LENA: Earl Montgomery Jones ...And he wanted to marry us...
LULU: Wanted to many Lena...They always want to marry Lena...
LENA: Not the High-boy...
LULU: So where is he now? Where is anybody now?
HOSS: *(Putting coffee on the table)* I'm here.
LULU: Lucky us...you and the Circus Bees...Let's look at the thermometer...

Lena and Lulu cross to the thermometer.

LULU: Then one evening High-boy got up on those big stilts of his and hiked off into the sunset. No note, *nothing*...I think he had the hots for the Bull Man.
LENA: He wasn't like that, Lulu.
LULU: They're all like that...
LENA: Not Earl...
LULU: Maybe not Earl...
LENA: Earl got down on his hands and knees and proposed to me old-fashioned style...
HOSS: So where is he now?
LULU: Where is everybody?
LENA: Got himself run off into the swamps...
LULU: And hanged himself...
HOSS: I thought you said he was John Law...
LULU: He was working for the Sheriffs office when we met him ...a sweet boy just out of high school...
LENA: I was seventeen then...
LULU: So was I, honey.
LENA: He came out to make sure that our show was going to Sunday School...
LULU: Of course we were just forty-milers then ...We didn't travel then, but if a show came around, Momma would be sure to stick us in it...
LENA: Afterwards, Earl started coming around the house ...Difficult to go out, of course, but we had our fun...
LULU: Of course, as soon as the local yokels found out that Earl was coming to see us in earnest, the good Baptists of the community rose up on their hind legs ...I mean they began screaming bloody murder...
LENA: They thought we were going to lure Earl into committing bigamy...
LULU: Well, you know two's company, but three's an orgy, and of course Earl's parents were fit to be tied...There was talk they were going to bum us out, so one night, Momma loaded us into a wagon of cornflakes and snuck us out of town before the thistle-chins reached the front door...
LENA: I don't know what they would have done to us...
LULU: Of course, it was all right as long as we were freaks, but as soon as it was serious...

LENA: Day and night they must have hounded Earl, because momma got this letter from a friend of hers saying that Earl had been taken off the force, and that he had run off into the swamps...Some of the farmers chased him there ...and he hadn't done nothing...
LULU: Then momma got this newspaper clipping saying they discovered him hanging from a tree ...Everybody figured he had done it himself...
HOSS: Well, I'm sorry...
LULU: You're sorry? (*snaps the locket shut)*...Ah, screw it...(*takes a badge from the night stand*) ...A friend sent us his cookie cutter.
LENA: Let's not talk about it anymore ...Make me another giraffe, will ya, Charlie?
HOSS: (Standing up) Wait till I get back...
LENA: Aw, Charlie...
HOSS: It won't take me too long ...How long does it take a man to say yes or no?...
LULU: Depends on the question...

Lena picks up the newspaper.

LENA: Then hand me the scissors...I want to cut out some ads.
LULU: I haven't even read it all yet..

Charlie hands Lena the scissors.

LENA: It's two weeks old...If you haven't read it by now, you never will.

Hoss puts on his hat, and takes up his rabbit's foot.

LULU: So? I move my lips.
HOSS: Wish me *luck...(shows* off *his red vest)* How do you like my new middle piece?
LENA: Sum, Charlie...It makes you look handsome...

Lulu takes up Amusement Business. Lena cuts out an ad from the newspaper.

HOSS: Won't take me long at all ...and it could be good for all of us...

Hoss exits.

LULU: Don't bring back any more Lot Lice with ya.

We hear the sounds of Charlie going quickly down the stairs. Lena quietly cuts ads out of her newspaper. Lulu stares at the closed door.

LIGHTS OUT.

END OF SCENE ONE.

SCENE TWO

It is growing toward evening. A breeze blows against the flimsy curtains on the window, blows the thermometer back and forth. The dirty dishes are still on the table. The bed has not been made. Lena and Lulu still sit in their original positions on the divan, where by now Lena has created a small pile of clippings. Lulu is still looking at Amusement Business, *though when the lights come up, it is obvious that we are in the middle of another dispute.*

LULU: He has a lot of nerve saying it would be good for us all.
LENA: It's just his way of spieling.
LULU: The broad-tosser knows exactly what he means.
LENA: Your guess is as good as mine.
LULU: Is it?
LENA: Sure. You hear the same things I hear...
LULU: You hear them differently.
LENA: What do you think he means by it? You're the one who wanted him to square the beef, didn't you?...
LULU: I know what you're thinking.
LENA: I know what you're thinking, too. I used to think it was an advantage, but I don't think so anymore. We're not growing the same way anymore.
LULU: What do you mean? We're both exposed to the same experiences.
LENA: Not exactly. You get the left side, I get the right. The experiences on the right are not the same as the experiences on the left.
LULU: What grinder put that in your head?
LENA: I just feel it's true.
LULU: What you feel to be true and what is true are two different things ...Let's close the window...
LENA: Why?
LULU: Because it's getting cold out, that's why.
LENA: I like it.
LULU: I'm more sensitive to weather than you.
LENA: You're getting to be such a hypochondriac, you ought to go around with the thermometer up your rectum.
LULU: I'm closing the window.

LENA: You always get your own way.
LULU: If I'm sick, it's because whatever your onion is driving away, it's driving in my direction.

Lulu and Lena get up and close the window.

LENA: Leave it slightly open at the bottom. I want some air in here.
LULU: It's going to rain.
LENA: I hope not. Charlie's going to get his new middle piece ruined.
LULU: He should have taken a round top with him.
LENA: If you're so good at predicting the weather, why didn't you tell him it was going to rain?
LULU: Even if I can predict, I just don't want to tell everybody ...people make such fun when you're wrong.
LENA: What a great weather forecaster you're going to make ...I'm going to tell the weather to some of you suckers and to some of you, I'm not...
LULU: Sister, I think it's time you and I had a little pipe-fest.
LENA: What about? Charlie?
LULU: Of course about Charlie.
LENA: He's going to be back soon.
LULU: Sure he is. He's probably throwing a string of coconuts on some cat food...
LENA: He went to be taken on. You know the Governor. He gives everybody a rough time ...even when he's only hiring a punk pusher.
LULU: Hoss is probably finding out that the Governor's show is chained to the rails...
LENA: Lulu, what do you have against Charlie? He's been a good egg...
LULU: Why shouldn't he be good? We've been running a personal grab joint for him.
LENA: He's done his share.
LULU: He's done his share all right. Every time he opens his yap, there's a fight going on.
LENA: You jump on everything he says.
LULU: Why shouldn't I?...Doesn't he want to drag you off to that glorified lint with him?...
LENA: He never said it...
LULU: He's thinking iL..He's hinting it...saying how he wants to meet

momma, or if he gets taken on, it will be good for us all
LENA: If you're so good at reading minds, why don't you open a mitt joint?
LULU: Banana Nose's mind is easy to read--it's only got one thing on it...
LENA: I think you're just being mean...
LULU: Maybe because what I get on the left side makes me mean...
LENA: You're jealous...
LULU: Take the Brown Cow...
LENA: You're not scaring Charlie off, Lulu ...Charlie don't scare easy.
LULU: Any camel punk could do it
LENA: Every time I show some interest in someone...
LULU: I suppose if he gets with it, you'll want us to go on the road with him ...no matter what dog and pony outfit he gets taken by...
LENA: The Governor ain't running no dog and pony outfit...
LULU: So that's what you're thinking ...that we should give all this up because some la-ti-da broad-tosser comes in blowing more steam than a horse piano...
LENA: Give all what up? When did this become the Waldorf Astoria all of a sudden?
LULU: Better than drugging from town to town while all the suckers come to gawk...Of course, we're the big draw, so maybe Hoss thinks he's going to be our Lucky Boy...
LENA: He's getting taken on by himself...
LULU: Then let him go... it's better we don't see him again...
LENA: Better for who?
LULU: For you, Lena. He's trying to knife us...
LENA: He's on the up and up...
LULU: All he thinks about is up and up...
LENA. It's all you pipe about
LULU: We're not hitching up with him...
LENA: He hasn't asked yet...
LULU: You can feel it in the air. ..it's like the weather...
LENA: You're no good at predicting that either ...Besides, it's not us he's going hitched to...It's me...
LULU: Fm just an innocent bystander ...a neutral observer .I'll carry the white flag to bed...
LENA: It will be like the way we planned with Earl ...that's all ...you get your place and we'll get ours...Well divide up the week ...we spend

sometime at my place and sometime at yours...And when you get yourself a John, it'll be all even...
LULU: I had a John once and you scared him off...
LENA: I had nothing to do with it...The High-boy went after anything in skins...
LULU: When I get through with Banana Nose, he wont come near you either...
LENA: You're not going to spoil this one for me, Lulu...This is our last chance for a normal life...
LULU: A normal life? Have you been hit on your skull with a tack hammer?
LENA: Normal for us...for us...for us...
LULU: Normal for us is not to be taken on by every seat man...
LENA: You stop it, Lulu...! love Charlie and Charlie wants us...
LULU: Well, if he wants you, he better find some way of cutting us apart, because he isn't getting us...I'm not putting up with that gorilla for the rest of my life...

Lena has been brandishing she scissors she has been using newspapers.

LENA: Then I'll cut us apart, then!
LULU: Stop fooling around with the scissors...
LENA: Everything I ever wanted, you took from me ...you even put Earl's picture in your locket..

Lena jabs Lulu with the scissors.

LULU: Lena!...
LENA: Neither of us are good enough for Charlie...
LULU: Lena, you cut me...
LENA: Fli do more than that.
LULU: Give me those scissors...
LENA: We're going to travel with Charlie, aren't we?
LULU: Lena the Hyena...

With her left hand, Lulu tries to block the jabs of !he scissors.

LENA: You promise me...

LULU: You're going to be sorry for this, Lena...Momma said don't play with...
LENA: Look out!

Lulu has lost her balance. her hand grasps for Lena's hair as they fall to the floor .. Silence.

LENA: Lulu, you all right?...Lulu?
LULU: (*in severe pain*) Oh, my God...

Lena pulls Lulu and herself to a vague sitting position and we see Lulu's stomach covered with blood.

LENA: Lulu, you'll be all right.
LULU: (*barely*) Momma told you not to fool with scissors.
LENA: Help!
LULU: (*barely*) Open he window!...Nobody can hear you with the window closed.
LENA: Help me get over there.
LULU: (*barely*) Bitch! I can't stand up.
LENA: Oh the blood!...the blood....
LULU: (barely) Lena the Hyena.
LENA: Help us crawl over there... It was your idea to close the window.

Lena tries to crawl toward the window but Lulu's added weight is too much for her.

LENA: You're not helping, Lulu...Baby, baby...Don't you know I wouldn't hurt you for the world?...It hurts me, too, Lulu...It hurts me, too...Goddamn it, why do they make the windows so far away?...Somebody help me!...

Lena manages to grasp one of the chairs.

LENA: Baby, it was only a pair of scissors...People don't die from scissors...Wake up, Lulu...look at all we've been through together...We can survive that too.

Lena lifts the chair slightly and begins banging it on the floor to attract the people who live underneath.

LENA: Mrs. Miller, are you home?..Listen to me down there! My sistet hurt, she's passed out...Call a doctor!

Lena listens, but there is no reply. Lena bangs the chair on the floor hysterically.

LENA: Goddamn you, why aren't you ever home?...Hang on, Lulu, you hang on...Charlie's got to be back soon...If we only had a phone, but you wouldn't let me get a phone, would you?...because of the men calling up all the time...See what jealousy gets you, Lulu?...Lulu the Zulu. Lulu the Zulu...

Lena tries crawling toward the window, dragging painfully her sister's body.

LENA: I don't want to die, Lulu...Shit, you're getting blood over everything, you dumb cluck...If I can get the sheet, we can clean it up, huh?...I can get the sheet. Damn it, Lulu, I have something to live for...What are you doing this to me for? (*calls out*) Charlie!

Lulu is dead weight, but Lena manages to reach the divan and frantically grasps for the sheets, bringing whatever else was on the bed down on top of them...

LENA: (out of breath) Here we are, Lulu...Now we just have to sit and wait for somebody to come.

Using the sheets, Lena tries to staunch the blood and to clean Lulu's face, arms, dress.

LENA: Such a pretty dress we had...Don't you worry, Lulu, somebody'll come...That's what we'll do, Lulu, we'll pretend...We're just sitting in the Freak Show, and the grinder is out front, and he's getting the suckers to come see us...See, they're all going to come see *us...(She makes the sign of the cross*)...Hail, Mary, full of grace, blessed art though among women and blessed is the fruit of thy womb, Jesus...Send, somebody up...Please...*(She makes the sign of the cross again)*...Water...If we, could get some water, Lulu, can't we stand up?...There's no way you can be dead...It's just the shock...Lulu...What's happening to you?...Tell me...Tell me...*(She bangs Lulu's head on the floor)*...Talk to me, you bitch...You're doing this to punish me, aren't you?... like you did my whole life...It wasn't my fault we were attached and momma didn't cut us apart...Why do you keep saying it's my fault?...Lulu...*(The last is almost a wail).*

SILENCE.

Lena manages to hold onto the edge of the divan for some balance.

LENA: Lulu, you want to hear something funny? This is going to make you laugh, Lulu...! just thought of something really funny...Suppose they bring me to trial...What are they going to charge me with? I mean, you and I are one...I committed suicide and I'm still alive to tell about it. Isn't that a stick, Lulu?...Lulu, goddamn you...My onion...

Lena searches the pockets of her dress for her onion. She finds it, holds it to Lulu's nose.

LENA: Breathe, baby, breathe…

Lena angrily throws the onion across the room.

LENA: Mrs. Miller, why aren't you home for supper like everybody else?...Charlie...You know, Lulu, this isn't the way it's supposed to be...It's supposed to be nice and calm, with angels singing...are there any angels, Lulu?...I imagine it like a beautiful blue lake, and we're walking across the water...Me and you and Jesus...and we're walking across the watcr...He takes my hand and we just separate...Lulu, you spoil everything for me...and Earl...Oh, Charlie, why don't you come home?...Lulu. you know how afraid of things I am...I don't want to be alone...You're lucky, Lulu, because I wanted to die first, because that way I wouldn't have to be alone for a second.

Lena finds Lulu's locket among the sheets.

LENA: You know what's going to happen, don't you, Lulu?...You don't have to be a mitt reader to know...Your High-boy is going to come back to you...He's going to walk up *those* stairs on stilts, and you and he are going to get hitched, and me and Charlie...in a big church with all our friends...and we're going to have our own houses...and we're going to go back and forth between our houses...and we'll have children...good strong normal children...I can see the whole thing, Lulu...We just have to hang on. Jt's not just an accident, Lulu...It's just that I have never been alone before So I don't know what it's like You're here, but you're not here a it's so cold...Lulu, if you get well, I promise you...I swear it ! We'll study weather forecasting, and we'll get our own show, and if Charlie don't like he can shove it...You're right about not wanting to travel around with all those mud operas and the gillies coming out to gawk at the freaks...You know what I'm going to do, Lulu?–I'm going to speed things up...We're going to crawl back 'to the scissors and I'm going to do to me what we did to you...You'd like that, wouldn't you, Lulu? If I had been on the other side, it would have been me–and what am I waiting for? I know I can't live much longer than you, but even a minute is much longer...

Lena tries to reach the scissors.

LENA: Lulu, why didn't you go on a diet like me? But no, you got to fill yourself tip with that Flookum until your teeth rot out.

Lena lies back down on the floor.

LENA: Lulu, what's it like to die?...Tell me it isn't so much...

We hear the sounds of footsteps on the stairs.

LENA: Lulu, listen Charlie's coming back...I know that gorilla's walk anywhere...Lulu, *listen...(calls)*...Charlie, Charlie...Hurry, oh, hurry...Lulu's hurt.

The door opens and we see Charlie, slightly wet from the rain. We can see, he has also had a few drinks to pass the day.

HOSS: May H. Joseph, and Jesus...Lena...Lulu...what the...
LENA: (*calmly*) Did we get taken on, Charlie?
HOSS: I'll get a doctor.
LENA: *(desperately)* No...No, don't leave me, Charlie...
HOSS: What do you mean? Look at yourself...Your sister...I'lI get some...
LENA: I ain't used to being alone!
HOSS: (*Comforting Lena, holding her)* Keep calm, Lena, that's the important thing...I'm going to go downstairs to the phone booth at the corner and ll be right back–We've got to get an ambulance...
LENA: I like being held by you, Charlie.
HOSS: You poor kid. How long ago did this happen?
LENA. I don't remember...Too long...Charlie, close the window...It's so cold in here..
HOSS: Honey, Listen. let me go....
LENA: It doesn't matter
HOSS: Don't talk nonsense...
LENA: If you leave me, Charlie, I'll kill myself...

Charlie returns to take the scissors...

LENA: Make me a giraffe, Charlie...Please, Charlie, please...a funny spotted girl out of those balloons of yours...

Charlie turns and runs down the stairs crying for help.. Lena and Lulu lie on the floor face-up. If there is a balloon animal nearby, Lena reaches for it.

LENA: A red one...a red spotted girl to hold in my arms, so when we got heaven, everyone will say, "ooooh."

LIGHTS OUT.

END OF PLAY.

PENGUINS

Time: October, 1957

We are in the office of Warren D. Warshow, the director of a noted zoo in Denver. Colorado. The furnishings are simple–A desk, two office chairs, a filing cabinet or two, and a coat-rack. At stage left is a lectern equipped with a small reading light. On the desk are a telephone, an intercom, and a large radio which is playing as the lights come up.

RADIO: And now this short item from *The New York Times*: Two old friends–one considerably older than the other–have been trying to take trout out of St. Louis Creek, 10,000 feet up in the Colorado Rockies, seventy miles from Denver. One, the younger is not a fisherman, but a cook. His flapjacks would blow away on the mountain wind if they were not so good as to be eaten before the calamity could occur. He rolls his trout (when caught) in a bag of gold corn meal, fires them to a delicate brown and recommends that they be eaten by nibbling first along the backbone...

The door to the office opens and in walks Warren D. Warshow, a slender man of 45, elegantly dressed in a gray business suit. He is followed by Conrad Alstock, a much younger and bit more informal person. Alstock too works at the zoo. Warshow crosses to the coat-rack and hangs up his overcoat.

RADIO: Under these pleasant circumstances the two fishermen may be able to forget for long moments that one of them is the President of the United States and that one of them used to be. Mr. Eisenhower and Mr. Hoover may fear that the world is going to the devil.

Warshow crosses to his desk, then indicates that his friend is to be seated.

WARSHOW (*snapping off the radio*): The world indeed is going to the devil.
ALSTOCK: And why? Because the stupidity of the human race is not to be believed.

WARSHOW: I prefer animals and I miss the days when I was at the South Pole studying penguins. Everything seemed more peaceful then.
ALSTOCK: What were you studying exactly?
WARSHOW: Whether or not penguins could ever learn to play the violin. It was a government-funded program.
ALSTOCK: And did your penguins learn to play the violin?
WARSHOW: We never found out. The air temperature was so cold that the strings kept snapping. Then we switched to simple band instruments such as tubas and glockenspiels and we taught them to march.
ALSTOCK: And that worked?
WARSHOW: Did it work? The penguins would have marched to Argentina if we hadn't stopped them. Of course, I exaggerate a bit, but the results were heartening enough for our federal grant to be renewed, but then an opening at this zoo came up, and I abandoned the arctic.

Cross-fade to a lectern. One of the world's authorities–Dr. Murry D. Levick–is in the middle of his lecture on penguins of the Antarctic.

DR. MURRAY D. LEVICK: In various places through the course of these pages, reference is made to the 'ecstatic' attitude of the penguins. This antic is gone through by both sexes and at various times through much more frequently during the actual breeding season. The bird rears its body upward and stretching up its neck in a perpendicular line, discharges a volley of guttural sounds straight at the un-responding heavens. At the same time the comic movements of its 'sound box' can be seen going on its throat. Why it does this I have never been able to make out, but it appears to be thrown into this ecstasy when it is pleased; in fact, the zoologist of the 'Porquoi Pas' expedition termed it the 'Chant de satisfaction." I suppose it may be likened to the crowing of a cock or the braying of an ass."

Lights down on Dr. Levick. In the darkness, we can hear the "Chant de Satisfaction" of numerous Adele penguins. Lights up on the zoo director's office.

ALSTOCK: What was that?

WARSHOW: If I remember correctly it's the cries of satisfaction coming from the penguin house. There was one female penguin I remember in particular. She emitted a cry that sounded like the braying of an ass whenever we slept together.
ALSTOCK: You slept with the penguins?
WARSHOW: Well, not the male ones...Don't look so shocked. We where in a region where there were no singles bars for thousands of miles...Which reminds me. Where's Marcia? She's supposed to help with the Secret Service agents today.
ALSTOCK: Oh, haven't you heard?
WARSHOW: About what?
ALSTOCK: Marcia.
WARSHOW: She all right?
ALSTOCK: Yes. But she received a call this week-end. She had to drive up to St; Louis Creek and stock the stream with trout.
WARSHOW: Stock the river with trout?
ALSTOCK: Rainbow trout. You don't think anyone in his right mind is going to allow a President and an ex-President to return from a fishing trip empty-handed, do you?

Warshow takes out a cigar, clips the end; then offers the box to Alstock.

ALSTOCK (*passing on the cigar*): And then there are all the photo opportunities. President Eisenhower and Hoover posing with a string of freshly caught trout.
WARSHOW: But why Marcia? Shouldn't stocking creeks be the province of the Fish and Game Commission?
ALSTOCK: Of course. But don't forget that Marcia is only on loan to us for six months from that commission.
WARSHOW: Will she be back in time for the President's visit?
ALSTOCK: The Fish and Game Commission said they needed her for three days.
WARSHOW: Three days! How long does it take to toss a fish into water?
ALSTOCK: It's also a long drive out and a long drive back.
WARSHOW: But the President and Mr. Hoover are scheduled to arrive a 5 PM today for a private tour.

ALSTOCK: I'll never understand why any person from Washington D.C needs to go out of his way to see a zoo.
WARSHOW: The head of our board–Charles Hurley–set the whole thing up. He feels the publicity will bring us millions in donations.
ALSTOCK: But security arrangements are already costing us an arm and a leg. And I received a memo this morning. We are asked to removed The Salvador Dali prints from the private dining room.
WARSHOW: Why must we remove the Dali prints? Our President is a painter.
ALSTOCK: The President may be confused by surrealism.
WARSHOW: How can he be confused by surrealism? He's a Republican.

Lights down.

ANNOUNCER'S VOICE: Lady's and Gentlemen, for your delectation and enjoyment–THE FOUR VIOLIN-PLAYING PENGUINS, MINUS ONE.

Lights up on three musicians in tuxedos. With fiddles or violins under their wings, they waddle in. indeed, they do resemble penguins.

PENGUIN #l: And now for the Marcel Duchamp song–"My Heart Belongs to Dada".

THE FOUR VIOLIN PLAYING PENGUINS–MINUS ONE *(singing)*:

Yes, our hearts belong to Dada, So Dada can't be bad
Yes, our hearts belongs to Dada,
Dada, Dada, Dada, Dada, Dada, Dada

But I want to warn you critics.
Though I know your heads can swell,
In fact, our hearts belong to Dali
'Cause our Dali–he paints–so well.

They each hold up a reproduction of the Dali painting removed from the zoo dining room. A bit of soft shoe.

PENGUIN #l: On the other hand, we have so many facts and statistics coming in on us from all sides, our hearts belong to data.

THE FOUR VIOLIN PLAYING PENGUINS—MINUS ONE (*singing*):

Yes, our hearts belong to Data, Such facts can't be bad
Yes, our hearts belongs to Data,
Data, Data, Data, Data, Data, Data

Lights out. Lights up on the office.

WARSHOW: What's that strange look on our face?
ALCOTT: Oh, something silly came to mind.

He hums a few bars of My Heart Belongs o Dada.

WARSHOW (*shuffles papers*): I can't believe how complicated life has become because some politicians want to visit our zoo.
ALCOTT: Certainly this Presidential visit could not have come at a worse time.
WARSHOW: Why is this the worst time?
ALSTOCK: It's the mating season. Many of the animals are in heat. Yesterday, a member of our board brought her two young children to the zoo and three baboons masturbated right in front of them.
WARSHOW (*rises and crosses to the window. Looks out*): Well, carrot-cuffing baboons should make an exquisite photo op for the president.
ALCOTT: Have you decided who will replace Marcia on the tour?
WARSHOW: What's wrong with your young secretary—Karen...What's her name?
ALCOTT: McLeavy.
WARSHOW: She can help out with the Secret Service, can't she?
ALCOTT: Well, there is one small problem with Karen.
WARSHOW: Which is?
ALCOTT: She doesn't wear any underwear.
WARSHOW: She doesn't wear any underwear?...Allow me to write this down, so I may contemplate the full allegorical significance of your jest.
ALCOTT: I'm not kidding.

WARSHOW: No panties?
ALCOTT: No panties.
WARSHOW: No brassiere?
ALCOTT: No brassiere.
WARSHOW: No nothing?
ALCOTT: No nothing.
WARSHOW: Ah.! I love the glory of the double negative. (*Writes on his yellow legal pad)* ...How long have you known this?
ALCOTT: Ever since I hired her. It was her best qualification.
WARSHOW: And you've kept this information to yourself?
ALCOTT: Well, everybody knows.
WARSHOW: Not everybody. I was not informed.
ALCOTT: These days you don't visit my office very much.
WARSHOW: Remind me to be more friendly. May I inquire just how do you know Miss McLeavy is suffering from an underclothing deficiency?
ALCOTT (*on the defensive*): All my actions toward her have been on the most professional level.
WARSHOW: I implied nothing.

Pause.

ALCOTT: She does a lot of filing.
WARSHOW (*writes on his yellow pad*): Does a lot of filing.
ALCOTT: Not everything that needs filing begins with the letter A. The low drawers require bending and stooping.
WARSHOW: Whose low drawers?
ALCOTT: I' m sorry I brought the subject up.
WARSHOW: I was beginning to wonder about your inordinate interest in Zebras and Zebus and every other Z animal over the last few weeks.
ALCOTT: Therefore, I don't think it's a good idea to ask Karen to be part of the President's escort service....if that's the term.... Not even an ex-president's.
WARSHOW: Photographers love to see Ike flashing his famous grin.
ALCOTT: Grin? Our President will be beaming ear to ear...
WARSHOW: Connie, tell your secretary to wear some undergarments...it's only for a few hours, Goddammit!

ALCOTT: I can't speak to her about it!...Marcia might have been able to, but we didn't plan ahead.
WARSHOW: You have to speak to her...Bring the subject up ...casually.
ALCOTT: Casually? Certainly...Ms. McLeavy, could you hold my calls and, while you're at it, pull on some underwear?
WARSHOW: You should have dealt with it on day one...or whenever you noticed the problem.
ALCOTT (*stands up*): I'm not getting paid enough to give up the one perk I have.
WARSHOW: Perk? Is that what you call it? A perk? Next time I'll have full-frontal nudity penned into the contracts.
ALCOTT: No need to get testy...
WARSHOW: No, No need at all. I should not get testy. I shouldn't be upset. After all, I've got a President and ex-President due to arrive in a few hours. Numerous animals are in heat; penguins emit nauseating cries for desperate couplings; baboons and monkeys and, for all I know, giraffes are masturbating in and out of trees, making Onan look like the biggest prude in the Old Testament; the woman I counted on to help me with the Secret Service is up in the mountains attaching trout to fishhooks until her dainty hands are covered with blisters and blood, and fish shit for all know; the woman I request to take Marcia's place is unfit for service because of a certain understatement in her dress code....Is there anything I left out?

Pause.

ALCOTT: Has Robert informed you about the coral snake problem?
WARSHOW: Coral snake problem? What coral snake problem?
ALCOTT: Since early this morning a coral snake has been missing from the snake house.
WARSHOW: Missing?
ALCOTT: Unaccounted for.
WARSHOW (*writes on his legal pad*): Missing will do... Fine. Now there's a chance the President of the United States will accidentally step on a deadly coral snake and get bitten? **PRESIDENT DIES ON VISIT TO COLORADO ZOO**...And what will that do to all our hopes for money pouring in? Can anything else go wrong?

The Intercom buzzer goes off loudly. Both men stare at the intercom as we cross-fade to Dr. Murry D. Levick, as he continues his lecture on penguins.

DR. MURRAY D. LEVICK: When starting to fight, the cocks sometimes peck at each other with their beaks, but always they very soon start to use their flippers, standing up to one another and raining in the blows with such rapidity as to make a sound which, in the words of Dr. Wilson, resembles that of a boy running and dragging his hoop-stick along with an iron paling. Soon they start 'in-fighting,' in which position one bird fights right-handed, the other left-handed; that is to say, one leans his left breast against his opponent, swinging in his blows with his right flippers, the other presenting his right breast and using his left flipper...

Light down on Dr. Levick. Light up on the office of the zoo director. Alcott and Warshow are still staring at the intercom. Warshow answers.

WARSHOW: What is it, Mrs. Cunningham?
VOICE OF MRS. CUNNINGHAM: Mr. Hurley to see you.
WARSHOW: Doesn't he know I'm preparing the walk-through with the Secret Service? I'll see him at the formal dinner.
VOICE OF MRS. CUNNINGHAM: He says it's extremely urgent...extremely,
WARSHOW (*sighs*): Very well. Tell him to wait just three minutes...(*to Alcott*) The President of the Board is here.
ALCOTT: What do you think he wants?
WARSHOW: Does he know about Ms. McLeavy's air-conditioned nightmare?
ALCOTT: I am certain he hasn't seen my assistant.
WARSHOW: Then he's heard about the coral snake.
ALCOTT: No. That's top secret. We haven't even informed the Secret Service for fear they'd cancel the visit.

Warshow pours whiskey onto his white handkerchief and places the handkerchief upon his forehead.

WARSHOW: Well, you know Charles Hurley. I'd say his politics are slightly to the right of Nazi Germany, so when he shows up here, out of the blue, there is going to be trouble.
ALCOTT: Do you want me to remain and act as back up?
WARSHOW: No, I need you to solve the coral snake problem. Find the coral snake; move the masturbating monkeys out of sight, then have a discussion with your secretary about SCM,
ALCOTT: SCM?
WARSHOW: Strategic Clothing Maneuvers. Then meet me back here at three with the entire staff so we can have a walk though.... A dress rehearsal, if I may use that term for any activity involving your Miss McLeavy.
ALCOTT (*anxious to leave*): See you at three.
WARSHOW: On your way out, please ask Mr. Hurley to come in.
ALCOTT: Certainly.

As Alcott exits, lights up on the three little penguins–minus two–and how they grew. We see Professor Levick seated upon a simple wooden chair. He plays a banjo and balances a penguin on one knee.

DR. LEVICK (*singing*):

"Oh Susanna,
Don't you cry for me,
For I'm goin' to Alabama
With a penguin on my knee."

PENGUIN: Wait! I'm going to make a pun.
DR. LEVICK: Ladeez and Gentlemen, Gwen the Penguin here is going to make a pun. You going to make a pun, Gwen?
PENGUIN: Pun, Gwen? Oh that's clever. Knock. Knock.
DR. LEVICK: Who's there?
PENGUIN: Eisenhower.
DR. LEVICK: Eisenhower who?
PENGUIN: I's an hour late for lunch.
DR, LEVICK: Oh, that's funny.
PENGUIN: I thought so.

DR. LEVICK: Just what goes on in the penguin house when our backs are turned?
PENGUIN: Wouldn't you like to know?

Cross-fade to the office. After all we have been here before. The chairman of the board. Mr. Charles Hurley, owner of Hurley Chemical Works, with fire in his eyes, enters. In anticipation of the formal dinner with President Eisenhower and Mr. Hoover, he is dressed in a tuxedo. He carries a slender report in a bright blue binder and slams it on the desk.

HURLEY: Just what is going on in the penguin house when our backs are turned?
WARSHOW: Excuse me?
HURLEY: This report. You think you were going to keep it from me?
WARSHOW (*picking up the folder*): This one?
HURLEY: You know exactly what I'm talking about.
WARSHOW (*reads*): "The Sexual Preferences of Certain Penguins in the Colorado Zoological Park"...It is a scientific study by Dennis Johnson, one of the young Ph.D. candidates on our staff. I didn't think it would be of much interest to non-scientists.
HURLEY: My father was a scientist. He worked for years to perfect the flying tank.
WARSHOW (*indicates that Hurley should be seated*): My mother was a dress maker.

Hurley sits.

HURLEY: But your mother did not raise millions of dollars for this zoo the way my parents did, and now I find (*picks up the report*) that 6 penguins–nearly 25 per cent–in our penguin house are queer...queer as three dollar bills!
WARSHOW: That might be true.
HURLEY: "Might be true"? You don't believe a report prepared by one of our own staff?
WARSHOW: Well, in truth, I just received a copy of the report a few days ago, and I have had my hands filled preparing for the Presidential visit which you so generously arranged.
HURLEY: Please don't patronize me!

WARSHOW: I wasn't patronizing you. The visit from a President and an ex-President is extremely important and will give our zoo international publicity.

HURLEY (*standing up*): What kind of international publicity will it be if we expose the president to perverted penguins!

WARSHOW: *Perverted Penguins.* Good alliteration there, Charles.

HURLEY: What's alliteration? Some perverted homosexual act?

WARSHOW: Have a cigar?

HURLEY: No. It is true that I am responsible for this Presidential visit. My wife, with the other members of the board, getting ready for the formal dinner.. But I'll call the whole visit off. By God, I shall. If word gets around that we're stocking our zoo with filthy birds, Church leaders will rise up against us. We'll be the first zoo in America to be featured on the cover of *Confidential Magazine.*

WARSHOW: We're not the only zoo in the world housing homosexual penguins. Similar studies are coming in from Japan, Mexico, and Italy.

HURLEY: I don't care what goes on with Japs, Spics, and Wops. I'm concerned with the Morals of my own backyard. On my watch, Eisenhower must not be exposed to sexual perversity. My God! It's enough we have to deal with Adlai Stevenson.

WARSHOW: We're not showing the report to the President, but I doubt if he would care less about the sexual orientation of our penguins.

HURLEY: That shows what you know about Presbyterians.

WARSHOW: You're a Presbyterian, and I know you.

HURLEY: And you know me well enough that I'm not going to condone panty-waist penguins in our zoo. I am ordering you to cut the penguin house out of the tour.

WARSHOW: The penguin house is the true highlight of our zoo.

HURLEY: Highlight? You've turned it into a peep show for degenerates.. What if people on the tour spot some of the penguins acting…well, acting swishy?

WARSHOW: Do you know how difficult it is for experts to tell a male penguin from a female penguin...Sometimes even the penguins themselves get confused.

HURLEY: We're not talking confusion. We're talking Communist Conspiracy. The Reds have planted queer penguins in our midst to destroy the fabric of American Life.
WASHOW: If a few confused penguins can destroy the fabric of our way of life, that fabric must be very fragile.
HURLEY: Have you no morals?
WARSHOW: Are my morals under question?
HURLEY: Get rid of the poofy pouting penguins. Before the President arrives, get rid of them.
WARSHOW: What?
HURLEY: You heard me. I don't want pansies pissing on my parade.
WARSHOW: Look, Charles, I understand your concerns. But what should I do with the "Poofy Pouting Penguins" –as you so eloquently put it?
HURLEY: Shoot them, for all I care!
WARSHOW: Okay, I'll march out the homosexual penguins–by the way, I know quite a bit about marching penguins, even if a few of them do walk a little funny…I'll blindfold them, and put them in front of a firing squad…Ready, Aim, Fire! What would happen to our zoo if the press saw that?...Perhaps it would be more picturesque if I hanged them from lampposts. "What's that up there?" "Oh, don't worry about it, Mr. President. It's just a bevy of well-hung penguins. "
HURLEY: You're taking like an idiot.
WARSHOW: Sorry.
HURLEY: I didn't say kill them out in the open. Poison the penguins in secret. Poison their fish and then mail the bodies back to Moscow where they belong.
WARSHOW: And how will the Secret Service Agents, who are in the penguin house as we speak, react if they see penguins keeling over from poisoned food? You don't think they would allow Eisenhower and Hoover to partake of your special dinner, do you?
HURLEY: We're serving steak, not fish.
WARSHOW: It's three o'clock, Charles. I have a walk through with the Secret Service.
HURLEY: Fine. Detour the President and Mr. Hoover away from your home-grown Sodom and Gomorrah. Make up some excuse why the penguin house has to be shut down. No electricity. A power failure…

WARSHOW: Any sudden change in plans now will look suspicious and will jeopardize the entire visit.
HURLEY: Go to the snake house first, linger there...then say–apologetically–"Mr. President, I'm so sorry. We have spent so much time looking at the coral snakes; we don't have time for the penguins. Dinner is waiting."
WARSHOW: I don't believe it will be possible to substitute the snake house for the penguin house.
HURLEY: Why not? According to Walter Winchell, politicians love snakes.
WARSHOW: To be completely honest with you, we have a problem with one of our snakes.
HURLEY: Don't tell me the snake is queer.
WARSHOW: Worse than queer.
HURLEY: Nothing worse than queer.
WARSHOW: Missing.
HURLEY: Missing? Missing is not worse than queer. (*Pause.*) What do you mean missing?
WARSHOW: One of the coral snakes is unaccounted for. But, I have my best workers on the problem at this moment,
HURLEY: You mean President Eisenhower is going to come here, take one look at communist brain-washed poofy penguins...he and Mr. Hoover are going to throw up, and while they're vomiting at the sight of Marxist perversions right in the middle of America, a coral snake is going to slither out of nowhere, and kill our beloved leader?...Not while I am Chairman of Board!.....Warren, clean out your desk. I want you and your penguin party out of here. You're plotting to kill our President!
WARSHOW: Charles, you know I am as loyal an American as you are. I'm not going to take any chances that anything bad is going to happen to our President...Nor an ex-president either.
HURLEY: A coral snake on the loose! This is the reptile that breaks the camel's back.
WARSHOW: The camels are as straight as they come. Of course, camels are not supposed to be straight. They are supposed to have humps.
HURLEY: After President Eisenhower and Mr. Hoover leave for Washington tonight...And by God they had better leave alive and in

one piece…You and I are going to sit down and have a long talk. As long as there is one swishy penguin in this zoo, you will not get one red cent from my foundation. Not a dime. And without my support, this zoo will go under faster than I can say "You're fired!". You understand?
WARSHOW (*humbled*): I understand.
HURLEY: The rest of the Board will back me. We've had it up to here with you and your Charles Darwin Godless ways….I've put my reputation on the line for this visit. It will go off without a hitch. Or you will go off. Do you understand me?
WARSHOW (*humbled*): I understand you.
HURLEY: Now I'm going back to oversee the dinner arrangements. Call me as soon as the coral snake problem is solved.

He start out, comes back.

HURLEY: And one more thing. I want the penguin house sealed. There will no longer be a Penguin House. I don't want my teen-aged sons corrupted by your Commie-leaning Antarctic recruitment tactics…You see? It is *your* morals that are under question.

Hurley exits, Warshow sinks down in his chair and pulls out a bottle of whiskey. The intercom buzzes.

VOICE OF MRS. CUNNINGHAM: Mr. Warshow?
WARSHOW: Yes?
VOICE OF MRS. CUNNINGHAM: The staff is assembled for the walk-through.

Lights out. Lights up on two penguins who waddle across the stage.

PENGUIN #1: How is the 31st President of the United States like a vacuum cleaner?
PENGUIN #2: They're both Hoovers?
PENGUIN #1: Naah. They're both vacuums.

Lights down. Spotlight on the radio in Warshow's office.

RADIO: The Soviet Union announced a few hours ago that it has successfully launched a man-made satellite into space. The orbit of the satellite, named Sputnik, is now orbiting about the earth at a height of some 560 miles above the earth and has a maximum speed of 18,000 miles per hour. The device is eight times heavier than the one the United States has planned to launch. The Soviets now claim the lead in science. Upon hearing the news, President Eisenhower, who has been on a fishing trip with ex-president Herbert Hoover, cut his vacation short and is flying back to Washington. We now return to our regular programming.

Music from the radio. The door to the office opens. Warshow and Alcott enter. Warshow crosses to the radio and turns off the music.

WARSHOW (*rubbing his hands in triumph, he turns back to Alcott*): Well, I thought the walk-through was a success.
ALCOTT (*agreeing*): A success. Definitely a success.
WARSHOW: The coral snake is back in the cage.
ALCOTT: That's a relief.
WARSHOW: A huge relief. It is a shame about Miss McLeavy, though.
ALCOTT: Yes.
WARSHOW: It was a good thing we had the snake serum on hand and a coral snake expert with us. Very fortunate indeed.
ALCOTT: .The coral snake biting Miss McLeavy like that when she thought she was picking up a brightly colored necklace.
WARSHOW: I wish we had seen the snake before she had.
ALCOTT: She blames the underwear. She claims snakes are attracted to silk fabrics.
WARSHOW: Not true.
ALCOTT: I believe she's planning a lawsuit...Twenty million dollars is the conservative figure.
WARSHOW: She just needs to calm down. We saved her life.
ALCOTT: We endangered it first.
WARSHOW: I told you to find the snake before the walk-through.
ALCOTT: I did the best I could. There was a chance it was dead.
WARSHOW: Call the florist and send Miss McLeavy the biggest arrangement of flowers they have.

ALCOTT: Very well. But you should have seen the look on the faces of the Secret Service men. One of them would have shot the snake had not Johnson had not jumped upon Miss Mcleavy.
WARSHOW: Bad form to shoot a snake when there's a snake expert in the house.
ALCOTT: But now the Secret Service has declared the snake house off limits and they want President Eisenhower and Mr. Hoover to spend more time with the Penguins.

A knock at the door.

WARSHOW: Who is it?
MALE VOICE: Secret Service.
WARSHOW: Come in.

The door is opened. Standing in the doorway is a Secret Service man.

SECRET SERVICE: Mr. Warshow?
WARSHOW: Yes?
SECRET SERVICE: I'm afraid I have some bad news, sir. It's about the scheduled visit; President Eisenhower is flying back to....

Lights down as the agent delivers the bad news.

LIGHTS OUT.

END OF PLAY.

PERCUSSION

Lights up on two men and one woman dressed in work clothes. They stand behind various boards and saw-horses and hammer away, creating percussive Rites of Spring.

MALE VOICE FROM OFF-STAGE: If you don't stop that infernal hammering, I'm going to shoot myself.
CARPENTER #l: That is very considerate of you, Sir. After all, we are building your coffin.
COFFIN BUILDER #1: Your coffin, your coffin. We're building your coffin.

The hammering builds, then softens. From offstage, we hear a gunshot.

COFFIN BUILDER #2: Of all the musical sections, percussion elicits the most irony.

Lights out. Lights up on a man in his early forties, seated on a low stool. He wears a brown suit, a colorful bow-tie, and eye-glasses.

YOUNG MAN: You're a young man and you meet this attractive young woman and all you want to do is get into bed with her. So you finally score, but one thing leads to another and you soon end up in a life you could never have possibly imagined. Not even if you were Dr. Seuss could you imagine it. Or Franz Kafka. You end up with lots of strange clutter in your life–like children. And soon there are all these responsibilities hammering your head and heart and soul. And you don't exactly know what happened, except you have this terrible headache, so you turn to Dr. Krankeit of Vaudeville fame.

The man on the stool swivels to Dr. Krankheit of Vaudeville fame. Dr. Krankeit is in a white gown and carries a large mallet and a slightly larger stethoscope.

DR. KRANKHEIT: Now, young man, just what seems to be wrong?
YOUNG MAN: I feel as if some one is hitting me on my head with a hammer.

Dr. Krankkeit hits the young man on the head with a hammer.

DR. KRANKHEIT: You mean like this?
YOUNG MAN: Well, no. Not exactly.

Dr. Krankheit hits him on the head again.

DR. KRANKHEIT: You mean like this then?
YOUNG MAN: No…Not exactly...May I try?
DR. KRANKHEIT: Of course not. You're not a doctor. Only a licensed medical practioner should hit you on the head like this.
YOUNG MAN: Well, I am a trained percussionist.
DR. KRANKHEIT: Yes? For what orchestra?
YOUNG MAN: The Royal Philharmonic, conducted by Albert Scarletti. I have two tickets for tonight's performance of Shostakovich, if you would like them.

The Doctor takes the tickets.

DR. KRANKHEIT: Thank you. I'll take my nurse. She was once engaged to the Cello player.
YOUNG MAN: But this headache is driving me mad.

Dr. Krankeit hits him on the head with a mallet.

YOUNG MAN: The tone sounded correct. You're getting closer to why I have a headache. Hit me one more time.
DR. KRANHEIT: Sorry. Your insurance covers only three hits per visit....(*CALLS OFF-STAGE*) Oh nurse!

The traditional buxom nurse enters, wearing nurse's white.

NURSE: You called, Doctor?
DR. KRANKHEIT: Yes. Prepare the patient for surgery.
YOUNG MAN (*jumps up*): Surgery? I only have a headache.
DR. KRANKHEIT: If you think you came in here with a headache, think about me operating on you. Then think about the whopping bill you're going to get. Now that will give you a real headache.

YOUNG MAN: I'm not being operated on without a second opinion.
DR. KRANKHEIT: Nurse, does this young man here need to be operated upon?
NURSE: Of course, doctor.
DR. KRANKHEIT: Now there's your second opinion...Now get undressed.
NURSE: Me, doctor?
DR. KRANKHEIT: No. I'm talking to the patient for once.
YOUNG MAN: You're crazy.
DR. KRANKHEIT: I'm crazy? What? I am supposed to pay the rent by selling you three aspirin? For God's sake, man, think of somebody besides yourself. Think of what I had to go through to get my degree.
YOUNG MAN: What did you go through?
DR. KRANKHEIT: Well, this nurse here for one....Plus three diploma mills. For that somebody has to pay. Health Care isn't merely a case of button, button, who's got the button.
NURSE: Oh I like that game.
DR. KRANKHEIT: Health Care is a fight to the finish. A struggle against all odds. And I lay you three to one we can cure this headache of yours. *(turns to the nurse)* As for you, young lady, I'll lay you (*pause*)....three to one that you can cure him on our own.
YOUNG MAN (*Interrupting. He stands up*): I am cured! The pounding has stopped. And I can walk. I can walk!
DR. KRANKHEIT: So what? You could walk when you came in here.
YOUNG MAN: I know. I am so grateful to leave with what I had.

Young man rushes out.

DR. KRANKHEIT: Nurse, call my HOM.
NURSE: Do you mean HMO?
DR. KRANKHEIT: What is this a spelling contest? No. I want to call home. H–O–M. The E and the QR are silent.... Oh., forget the phone call.

Dr.Krankheit embraces the nurse. Lights out. We hear the sound of horses' hooves as provided by old-time radio sound effects; coconut shells might do the trick.

VOICE OFF: "And the cry of Hi-Ho Silver. And now we take you back to the thrilling days of yesteryear and/or the thrilling years of yesterday."

Lights up on the young man from the previous scene crossing to a coat stand from which hangs a Stetson hat and a gun (cap pistol) in a holster. The young man straps on the cap pistol, then he puts on his ten gallon hat.

YOUNG MAN: When I was 8 or 9 years old I received perhaps the best birthday present I ever received or ever will receive–a cap pistol with a holster and belt. The gun was modeled on the kind used by Hopalong Cassidy, and when I strapped on the holster I felt important. I felt I could handle any situation that would come my way. Day after day I practiced my quick draw. (*He demonstrates.*) But what I remember most is the smell of the caps after they had been fired. The caps came in tiny coils. Sometimes 6 to a box. Sometimes in no box at all. A child loading caps into the bullet…
YOUNG MAN (*continued):* chamber experienced a great sense of competence. It was a bit like loading film into your own camera. Modern children, because of computers, video games, and political correctness no longer enjoy cap pistols. In a world of losses, it is just one more loss. You loaded the gun with red strips of paper that contain small squares. In the center of each square was a black dot containing, I suppose, gunpowder. (*HE AIMS HIS PISTOL STRAIGHT AT THE AUDIECE.*) You pulled the trigger. (H*E PULLS THE TRIGGER. A CAP GOES OFF.*) In one smooth percussive stroke, the hammer of the gun fell against the black dot and a loud noise was heard, followed by a burning, acrid smell. Then a small and tender wisp of smoke. What wouldn't I give today to recapture such ecstasy? I swear that if a woman really wants to seduce a man she should wear a perfume called CAP PISTOL De la NUIT. The man would become putty in her hands in no time. As for music...well, there was that summer when I was in fourth grade when Spike Jones and his band came to play in our school auditorium. He twirled his bass fiddle around and around, then pulled out a cap pistol, perhaps two cap pistols, and fired into the air. It was at that moment that my love for classical music began.

He fires off another shot from his cap pistol.

YOUNG MAN (*sings, ala PORGY AND BESS*): Shostakovich! You is my woman now! You is...etc.

Lights out. In the darkness, we hear a symphony concert in progress. A full orchestra plays a Shostakovich symphony and we are in the passages where percussion is emphasized. We listen for a minute or two, then lights up. We see a middle-aged woman in an elegant peignoir seated at a small breakfast table. She is eating walnuts.. She smashes the walnuts, one-by-one, with a tiny mallet, then she sifts through the pieces for the kernels. Enter Albert Scarletti, a tall, elegant, middle-aged man dressed in a tuxedo, complete with a cape. He crosses to the coat stand, where now hangs–once again–the pistol and holster. He puzzles over it, then hangs up his cloak.

GEORGINA: Dear Albert, You were out all night.
ALBERT: I know. After last night's concert at Albert Hall, I could not bring myself to return to civilization. I am in deep despair...suicidal, if you will.
GEORGINA: Was it as bad as all that?
ALBERT: Horrible. Simply horrible. Have you noticed that as music grows more and more atonal, violence in society increases...I really should draw up a graph on the subject.
GEORGINA: But weren't you conducting Beethoven's Fugue for Two Oboes and a Wurlitizer...I know because I attended the open rehearsal....

Albert takes his usual place in the breakfast nook.

ALBERT: Not Wurlitzer. A howitzer is more likely.
GEORGINA (*Flattens a walnut*): Would you like some toast?
ALBERT: No, thank you. After last night's concert, I'll need something imported...Such as hemlock from Greece...May I help myself to the bacon?
GEORGINA: Go right ahead. I'll signal the maid to bring strong coffee.

Georgina gets up, crosses to a. J. Arthur Rank Gong. She strikes Gong with a mallet, then returns to her walnuts.

ALBERT: Last night, in the middle of *Shostokovitch's Sixth,* the percussionist got carried away. He wouldn't stop his infernal pounding on the kettle drums. He was like a man possessed, as if a malignant spirit had overtaken him. He was like a maniac....no doubt a student of Postmodernism. But once he started pounding, he would not stop. He completely over-rode the score. The phrase *poco allegro* might as well have been a foreign language to him.
GEORGIA: But *poco allegro* is a foreign language, dear.
ALBERT: I know that, but it wasn't Italian in the score he was following. It was a secret code. He was pounding away on the drums as if he were signaling life on another planet. In fact, invasion by creatures from Mars would have improved the evening appreciably.

The maid (played by the same voluptuous woman who was the nurse in the Krankheit sketch) enters. This time she is in a maid's outfit.

MAID: You rang?
GEORGINA: My brother desires coffee.
ALBERT: And a cyanide capsule.
MAID: And does the master desire anything else.
GEORGINA: Yes. But I'm not going to open that can of worms.
MAID: Good. Coffee, a cyanide capsule, and a can of worms.

She exits.

GEORGINA: What did you do?
ALBERT: I tried to wave the madman off, waving my arms left and right, up and down, then around and around like an egg-beater in heat. Of course, the rest of the orchestra had come to a screeching halt. There was no way that two flutes were going to be heard over the Tympanum.
GEORGINA: You poor man. What did you do next?
ALBERT: I reached into his coat pocket and pulled forth a revolver -- a Smith and Wesson, I believe...or, because it was a symphony, perhaps it was a Steinway...In any case, I pointed the revolver at the percussionist and shouted for all to hear, "Stop, or I'll shoot."
GEORGINA: Is the percussionist the son of a friend of ours?
ALBERT: Not any more.

GEORGIA: Of course, he is. He's from the Gottfried Estate. Suffers from terrible headaches, his mother says...So, what young Gottfried do? Did he stop?

ALBERT: No. He merely switched to the triangle. Did you ever see one of those God-awful American westerns where the cook calls the cowhands to supper? A chow-down, I believe it is called, in the vernacular. The cook beats the triangle to a fare-thee-well with a large spoon and cows, cacti, and drooling field hands come running. Well, young Gottfried's triangular convulsions sounded so much worse than any Hollywood western.

GEORGINA: So what did you do then?

ALBERT: I fired at him.

GEORGINA: Gottfried was fired? Well, I'm certain he deserved it. Acting like a young fool. Although I understand that becoming a professional musician is detrimental to anybody's character.

ALBERT: No. I mean I fired. I shot the percussionist.

GEORGINA: You shot Gottfried?

ALBERT: Well, technically I shot at Gottfried. Scarletti is a conductor of symphonies, not a marksman...I missed. The bullet ricocheted off the gong and entered the chest of the Queen Dowager who happened to be sitting in the front row. A massive chest, I might add. She died instantly. Or, if not instantly, at least in a timely fashion.

GEORGINA: You killed our Queen Dowager? Isn't that against the law?

ALBERT: It was an accident. I certainly didn't do it on purpose.

GEORGINA: At your age you should know better not to make a large gong a part of the orchestra. It makes it far too easy for a bullet to ricochet off it.

ALBERTA: A conductor cannot prepare for every contingency.

GEORGINA: Well, did the percussionist–seeing that the bullet meant for him had brought down our Queen Dowager–refrain from outburst?

ALBERT: Seeing the dead queen sprawling in her seat like a beached whale, he took up the drums and launched into the Royal funeral march. I had no choice. I fired a second time. At this point, the audience began to suspect that the pistol shots were part of Shostakovich's score and that the shooting of the Queen Dowager was merely performance art.

GEORGINA: So, much passes for art these days.

ALBERT (*continues his breakfast*): That's why public funding for the arts is such tricky business.

GEORGINA: Did your second shot bring young Gottfried down?

ALBERT: Like a pregnant gazelle. The second time worked like a charm. The percussionist clutched his chest and cried out for all to hear: "The capital of Micronesia is Yapase." And then he died, falling on his drums, producing one last disgusting thud.

GEORGINA: "The capital of Micronesia is Yapase" That's curious.

ALBERT: He wanted to end his day on an educational note. But, of course, the capital of Micronesia is Palikir, not Yapase. So he was wrong about that too. Drumming is not good for the brain. Everyone says so.

GEORGINA: And did the concert continue?

ALBERT: Well, not exactly. The shooting of a performer and an audience member who was probably a season subscriber provided a prolonged caesura, if you will. I suppose I could have returned to the beginning of the movement, but that would have required recruiting a percussionist from the audience and who could know if the musician's union would approve. Besides, most of the other musicians were hiding under their chairs. The violinists had tied white handkerchiefs to their bows and were waving them in the air, pleading for a cease fire.

GEORGINA: I hope the concert wasn't being broadcast by the BBC. It reflects so badly upon the state of our culture.

ALBERT: The first cello player, however, must have been a friend of the dead percussionist, because he picked up his bow and threatened to stab me.

GEORGINA: No, dear Albert. No.

ALBERT: Yes, dear Georgina. But, as you know, because of my superior musical training I am well versed in the bowing movements of rabid cello players. I sidestepped the thrust. I quickly picked up my baton and, reenacting dueling scenes from several Basil Rathbone movies, we dueled frantically back and forth across the stage. Cutting, slashing, thrusting, parrying. Not always in that order, of course.

GEORGINA: Modern sport is more confusing than Russian music.

ALBERT: At the same time the audience was, as you can well imagine, getting restless, I was trying to decide that if I was not going to play the remainder of the programme, whether they should demand a full refund.

GEORGINA: Oh, Albert. You are infuriating. What was the outcome of the duel? Were you cut to ribbons?
ALBERT: Not a scratch on me. Unfortunately, the musicians, who were lying on the floor and who were getting a birds-eye view of the action, saw me waving my baton madly and it dawned on them that I might be calling on them to play something by Stravinsky. Thus, there was a mad scampering to see if they could locate the score. In the meantime, my right arm was getting tired and, since I was ten to fifteen years older than the cello player...well, I merely pulled out my revolver again and shot the cello player between the eyes.
GEORGINA: Not very sporting of you.
ALBERT: I agree. The audience started to boo to show its displeasure. Believe me...Someone will write a letter to the *Times.* But I have to keep in shape for tomorrow night's concert.
GEORGINA: It will not be easy top replace both a cello player and a percussionist so soon.
ALBERT: And the harpist.
GEORGINA: The harpist? But, Albert, you didn't say anything about the harpist.
ALBERT: Didn't I? Well, during the duel, the poor harpist had been lying face down on the floor and I accidentally stepped on her hand and crushed four fingers. She may never play again.
GEORGINA: I hope she has insurance for that sort of thing.
ALBERT: I'm not certain it is the kind of thing that ever gets written into policies. Insurance agents are so much more clever than classical musicians. Rock stars, perhaps, are as clever. Classical musicians, no.

Sounds of police sirens.

GEORGINA: Sounds like police sirens, dear Albert.
ALBERT: I suppose Scotland Yard will be here any minute. They were an infernal nuisance about the dead Queen.
GEORGINA: Oh people have to know everything these days.

The maid enters carrying her silver tray.

MAID: Your coffee, sir.
ALBERT: Carlotta, I thought you had forgotten all about me.

MAID: Sorry, sir, but I couldn't locate those other items you wanted. Will you accept your father's dueling pistol in place of the cyanide capsule?
ALBERT: Very well.
MAID: Also there are two men at the front door who wish to speak to you. They say they are from Scotland Yard.
ALBERT: Ask them to wait in the study. I'll be in presently.
MAID: Very well, sir.

He takes the dueling pistol from the tray; we hear the hammering sounds of carpenters working offstage.

ALBERT: But you may pour the coffee before you go....The dueling pistol was once used by my father in a production of *Hedda Gabler.*
GEORGINA: Really. What part did your father play?
ALBERT: He played Hedda...Absolutely ruined his career....(*he turns to the main*).He ended up performing embarrassing doctor sketches in vaudeville...Carlotta, what is that infernal hammering?
MAID: Some laborers are constructing a fence for the garden, I think.
ALBERT (*To Georgina*): Georgina, did you order the construction of a fence?
GEORGINA: Not that I remember and I believe I would remember that sort of thing.
ALBERT: What's going on?

He crosses to the window and shouts out.

ALBERT: If you don't stop that infernal hammering, I'm going to shoot myself.
VOICE FROM OFFSTAGE: That is very considerate of you, Sir. After all, we are building your coffin.

The hammering builds, then softens.

ALBERT: That does it! First, Shostakovich. Now this! My nerves are frazzled.

He puts the dueling pistol to his temple.

GEORGINA AND MAID TOGETHER: Albert. PLEASE, SIR, don't!

LIGHTS OUT.

END OF PLAY.

NIGHT FISHING IN THE ANTIBES

Two men (Manuel and Marsh) are kneeling downstage. They are peering into a river we do not see. They carry with them brightly colored fishing gear. Manuel carries a spear; Marsh carries a lantern and a net. Both men are dressed in white pants, white shirts, and rope sandals. Manuel is in his mid-thirties. Marsh is an older man, with gray hair. Upstage are two young, attractive women (Juanita and Cecilia) in brightly-colored skirts and blouses. The women stand on a bridge, where a bicycle is parked. With handkerchiefs, they wave and call to the men. Until they come down to the men, the women parade back and forth upon the bridge. Juanita and Cecilia eat vanilla ice cream cones.

MANUEL: Juanita and Cecilia want us to come up to them.
MARSH: Come up to them?
MANUEL: Sleep with them.
MARSH: Ah! Your euphemisms are marvelous. Sleep is it? What will you be dreaming in such a sleep?
MANUEL: You know what I mean.
MARSH: I never know what anything means, but I know what everything costs...Hold the lantern closer.
MANUEL: Cecelia said tonight is for Free.
MARSH: Free? It must be a very slow night.
MANUEL: Actually it is a very fast night. Everything is just where it should be and moving at he right speed. The moon shining overhead. The black river with its many breathing creatures. And women on the bridge, women filled with desire. Who dare ask for a more perfect night?
MARSH: Keep your mind on your work.
MANUEL (*unwinds the net*): Why is it that when I up here, when I am talking up here, you are thinking down there? I'm a young man; I could use a night off.
MARSH: I don't think up or down. I think sideways...
MANUEL: Yes. Think like a crab. And you live like a crab....Women don't have much use for a man who lives like a crab. Too much sideways, not enough in and out.
MARSH: When I see the kinds of men women do have use for, it makes my head spin with wonder.

MANUEL: They like us. They admire how night after night we bring home the big fish, the biggest fish in all of Antibes....That's why they're offering us a special rate. It's better than a special rate. Free.
MARSH: Take it from an old man. It's better to pay for everything now rather than later.
MANUEL: Free? How can it be cheaper than free?
MARSH: You're young, you'll learn the answer to that question much later in life. It's cheaper in the long run, and, in life, everything's for the long run.
MANUEL: If we don't go up to the bridge, there won't be any now or later.
MARSH: There is always a later. Adam's first word in Paradise was "Later."
MANUEL: Haven't we caught enough?
MARSH: If you really want to catch something, go with the women on the bridge. They'll give you something you'll never forget.
MANUEL: You are not a nice man.
MARSH: No. I am an old man. There's a difference. When you grow old it is more difficult to be nice. Less reason to, because you think to yourself 'What difference does it make? What difference does anything make? It's all bullshit.' Hold the lantern closer.
MANUEL: What is there to see?
MARSH: I don't know. I have been coming to this same river for over thirty years, and I still don't know what there is to see. Just as man sleeps with the same woman for year after year, there is always some essential part of her that eludes him. The same is true with rivers.
Some essential part of this river eludes me.
MANUEL: How would you know? You haven't slept with a woman in how many years?
MARSH: It's like riding a bicycle. Once you learn you never forget.... You just get on and pedal.
MANUEL: I think your technique leaves something to be desired.
MARSH: I suppose. I am a student of rivers and oceans, not women. Better to be the one with the spear than the one who gets hooked.
MANUEL: Tell me...Do you think it's possible to make love on a bicycle?
MARSH: Possible, but not desirable. You see a bicycle is essentially a chastity belt with wheels. That's why you always see the village priest

riding on them. It's the pressure of the bicycle seat on the testicles that acts as a kind of contraceptive.
MANUEL: Stop! You are making my head hurt. No wonder you can't get any one to fish with you...You don't need a spear. You talk the fish to death.
MARSH: A bicycle is essentially pure because it does on two wheels what Death does at night–gets people from one place to another without a lot of extras.
MANUEL: You shouldn't have been a night fisherman. You should have been one of those men who stand in the city square, waving your arms, and preaching about free love or the meaning of life. Up comes an empty net, down goes a sermon.
MARSH: In China, I bet there are so many bicycles that if they were lined up end to end, they could reach from here to the moon.
MANUEL: I am sorry that I me mentioned the bicycle. Can we talk about something else? You mentioned the moon, look at the moon. See how it floods the landscape. Nearly everything is washed pure white.
MARSH: Tonight, I can tell, you are not in the mood to fish.
MANUEL: No, I am not. Can I piss on the lantern and go off with the whores?
MARSH: Put the lantern down right here next to me, and go piss on your toes....leave me the net....Now go. Enjoy the free ride on the best mountain there is.
MANUEL: I'll be back in an hour.
MARSH: Don't flatter yourself. It won't take that long.
MANUEL: I am not like you, speedy Gonzalez.
MARSH: All right, don't hurry.
MANUEL: Will you be here when I get back?
MARSH: Where am I going? What else have I done with my life, but spend every moment of it here...waiting...listening.

Manuel goes up to the bridge. We see him greet Juanita. They exchange a few words we do not hear. Marsh has returned to his fishing. Cecelia comes down from the bridge and watches Marsh at work. She holds out her ice-cream cone.

CECILIA: Want to eat something?
MARSH (*gruff*): What do you have in mind?

CECILIA: You're not a nice man.
MARSH: You just discovering that?
CECILIA: I don't think I can finish all this ice-cream all by myself. It's melting all over me.
MARSH: I'm certain there are young men around willing to melt all over you.
CECILIA: Tonight's my night off.
MARSH: So I have heard.
CECILIA: Tonight's everything's on the house. Why I wouldn't be surprised that if we walked into town, the owners of the shops would be rushing out into the street to give us everything they own. Bouquets. Bottles of Wine. Tortoise shell combs. I got this ice-cream cone, for free....Well, not exactly for free. I had to go into the bushes with Mr. Morales. But I didn't have to pay for it. That's what I mean for free. After all, it is an ice-cream cone…What I did to get the bicycle would make you sit up and take notice. (*Pause.*) I guess everybody must get something in exchange, or where would all the little fishes come from....

Marsh tosses his spear into the stream, but comes up empty.

CECILIA: Don't you ever take a break?
MARSH: For what?
CECILIA: To take advantage of things...Just to sit back and enjoy life
MARSH: No. I sit up and take notice.
CECILIA: You must have missed a lot of life just sitting around here. A lot of pleasures.
MARSH: I am sure I have.
CECILIA: A lot of pleasures in this life.
MARSH: There are. But there are only so many hours to a day. Or night.
CECILIA: A fish is just a fish. You eat them. You toss away the bones. My grandfather said the bones make good fertilizer.
MARSH: Dead people too.
CECILIA: You're getting too morbid in your old age. Soon nobody will come down from the bridge to talk to you. The trouble with me is that I am too nice.
MARSH: Sit up, sit down, sit back, sit up, sit around; your work is your work, and my work is my work.
CECILIA: A shame.

MARSH: Why a shame?

CECILIA: There must be more to life than tossing big spears at tiny fish.

MARSH: Sometime the fish are not so tiny.

CECILIA: I have seen some of the big fish.

MARSH: And sometimes the fish talk to me.

CECILIA: You mean you understand the language of fish?

MARSH: I didn't say I understand. But they talk to me.

CECILIA: And what do the fish say?

MARSH: Kush...Kush...Kush....

CECILIA: Kush....Kush..Kush? Some conversation that is. No wonder all fishermen are crazy.

MARSH: I said they talk to me. I didn't say it was a conversation.

CECILIA: Am I really hearing this? Believe me; I have better things to do with my time than to worry about the language of fish.

MARSH: Then do it.

CECILIA: Why are you so mean?

MARSH: Because the good die young. Kush. Kush.

CECILIA: What do you think Kush means?

MARSH: I know what it means. It means that even on a night when everything is free, from moonlight on down, you pay for it through your teeth.

CECILIA: And so what does it gain you to spend your time listening to dumb fish mouthing off? Me? I prefer it when my customers don't talk. Their breath is bad enough.

MARSH: Fish are not exactly customers.

CECILIA: Close enough.

MARSH: When they speak it means I have to work all that much harder to hold on.

CECILIA: Same here. Drains all the fun out of the good moments.

MARSH (*tosses his net into the dark river*): Maybe you're right.

CECILIA: About what?

MARSH: About everything.

CECILIA: I can't be right about everything. I didn't even finish school.

MARSH: When I first started fishing, on my own I thought I was doing it for the thrill of it. To bring back those moments when my father had taught me about night fishing.

CECILIA: Of course I could be right about some things. For example, eating an ice cream cone on a hot summer night is not too bad.

MARSH: My pyramid would be my skill with the spear in dark water. The years passed, and every night I came down here I thought I was doing it for the money. I had to make a living, support myself, keep a roof over my head, plan for the future, and then the future came and I still didn't have a pot to piss in and the big fish all got away. At least the biggest of them. And then I decided maybe I was working just to keep from being bored. To get through the day with a bit of dignity. "In the sweat of thy face shalt thou eat bread, till thou return unto the ground; for out of it was thou taken; for dust thou art, and unto dust thou return."

CECILIA: You certainly know how to cheer a woman up.

MARSH: Genesis, Chapter Three, Verse something or other.

CECILIA: I thought so. I knew you couldn't make stuff like that up.

MARSH: It's from the Bible. Genesis refers to the Bible.

CECILIA: I had a Bible once. A friend gave it to me....Well, I did have to go into the bushes with him and lift my skirts, but I at least got a free book out of it. I didn't have to pay for it. That's what I mean by free. A thick book.

MARSH: You should have read it.

CECILIA: I started it. But I don't read books about snakes. Real life has enough snakes. But then I discovered something else. I discovered every motel room on the island has a Bible in it. No need for me to even worry about carrying one around.

MARSH (*pulls in his empty net*): Some day I thought I would catch Leviathan, the biggest fish of them all. Have everyone in the village stand about in astonishment at a young man with an old man's skill. Then later I thought about living forever through one's efforts, like the old Egyptian pharaohs building their pyramids. Then I thought of bringing riches home to my parents. My mother had nothing her entire life and the poverty made her bitter. I had parents who were miserably unhappy, and that made me bitter. The only way I can deal with the bitterness is to walk away from everything that makes the least demand upon me. When I the fish start talking to me too much is when I walk away.

CECILIA: Like you could walk way from your own skin.

MARSH: Night fishing is too demanding.

CECILIA: Well, my kind of night fishing is demanding too.

MARSH (*takes up a fishing spear*): Possibly....But all this work just didn't come out of nowhere. We have planets to build.
CECILIA: It's all imagination anyway. Why the other morning I was looking at a large blue plate in a store window, and I started to pretend what it would be like to walk right into the scene, wander under the blue willows, cross the blue china bridge into a unknown country. My brothers used to say that if you dug deep enough, you would dig all the way to China...What are you doing?
MARSH: Waiting to spear a big fish.
CECILIA: Can I try it?
MARSH: No. You won't like it.
CECILIA: Why not?
MARSH: Because it requires exquisite timing. You have to wait until the very last moment before you let go.
CECILIA: And you think I don't know how to do that? Ask any man in the village...Let me try it, please? After all, I came all the way down from the bridge to keep you company.
MARSH (*relinquishes the spear*): All right. I'll hold the lantern.
CECILIA: I bet I can spear a bigger fish than you.
MARSH: There's no substitute for luck in this world. I have seen people work all their lives and come up with nothing.
CECELIA: So what? Someday the universe will be no more. So everything will be equal. The rich and the poor.
MARSH: How do you know that?
CECILIA: Sometimes my customers tell me things.
MARSH: I bet.
CECILIA: Sex isn't the same for everybody.
MARSH: No argument from me.
CECILIA: I think I see something.
MARSH: Shhh!....I'll tell you when.
CECILIA: Now?
MARSH: Now!

Cecilia lunges at the fish. She comes up empty.

CECILIA: I missed.
MARSH: It's not as easy as it looks.
CECLIA: That was fun.

MARSH: You missed.
CECILIA: I know I missed. I'm not stupid. I know when I miss.
MARSH: I'm just telling you that you missed.
CECILIA: Turning into Johnny One–Note, aren't you? Well, let me tell you all the things you have missed. Did you see that shooting star over the mountains?
MARSH: What shooting star?
CECILIA: See?
MARSH: What mountains?
CECILIA: You need to raise your head once awhile.
MARSH: Perhaps I would see more stars if I had a job that allowed me to lie on my back.
CECILIA: You don't know how difficult it is for me to keep my eyes open.
MARSH: I'm tired. You don't know how difficult it is for me to keep my eyes open.
CECILIA: Maybe we should both quit working.
MARSH: Where would we be without something to do to fill our days? God created the world, but we must keep adding to it–fish, spears, fishing nets…
CECILIA: So where would we be if it were finished?
MARSH: I don't know.
CECILIA: Let me try again.
MARSH: No, you're right. Let's put away the fishing gear and go back to my place.
CECILIA: When did I say that?
MARSH: You have been saying it all night, haven't you?
CECILIA: Not when I'm getting the hang of spear fishing.
MARSH: Maybe you didn't notice, but you haven't got the hang spear fishing. You're not even holding the spear correctly.
CECILIA: Then teach me.
MARSH: This isn't a game! This is my life's work.... I fish in peace. So come on. Give me what you promised.
CECILIA: Quiet....I am going to spear a big fish.
MARSH: You think you're just going to walk down here from the bridge, take my place and spear the big fish?
CECILIA: You said there is no substitute for luck.

MARSH: But it's luck you have to be prepared for. I have spent my whole life preparing for what little luck I've got.
CECILIA: Show my how to do it.
MARSH: Teach yourself, the way I did....And when the big fish start chanting *kush, kush, kush*...Beware! I won't be around to help you.
CECILIA: Kush kush kush yourself.....Where are you going?
MARSH (*Crossing up to the bridge*): Off to have some fun. Isn't that what you want me to do? I'll get some rum and some women and let the world go....

Marsh exits. Cecilia tends to her fishing.

CECILIA: Men...What strange creatures they are. You need more than a spear and a net when you go hunting them....Even if you do catch them all you want to do is throw them back.

Juanita and Manuel return, just a bit worse for wear.

MANUEL: Marsh, we have come back for you.....

Manuel looks about.

MANUEL: Where is Marsh?
CECILIA: Gone off to have a good time...
MANUEL: Right. The old man never had a good time in his whole life. (*To Juanita*) He's gone loco. Thinks the fish talk to him.
CECILIA: I'm taking his place.
MANUEL: Taking his place?
CECILIA: Quiet....I hear something in the river.
MANUEL: No...No...Everything's wrong. What is this world coming too? (*Calls*) Marsh, come back...Just because I went away for a few minutes of fun, it doesn't mean we have to toss everything away....
JUANITA: What's wrong with men? Don't they know what they want?
CECILIA: Shhh!...
JUANITA: Work or play. Nothing seems to satisfy them.
CECILIA: Quiet...Can't you see I'm working?...

JUANITA: But it's supposed to be our night off. And tonight everything's suppose to be free...Why does everything get ruined? I like things the way they are. Why does everything have to change?
CECILIA: Bring the lantern over here.
JUANITA (*picks up the lantern*): Smells like piss, like someone has pissed on the fishing net. That's another thing wrong with men. They piss all over themselves.

Cecilia stabs the black water with her fishing spear.

CECILIA: I've got one... A big one...I think I've got him!
JUANITA: Let me see....Does this mean we're going to take up fishing?
CECILIA: I don't know what it means. I'm a whore, not a fortune teller.
JUANITA: Fishing at night?
CECILIA: No matter what we do....*kush...kush*.
JUANITA: What's wrong with the daylight when you can see what you're doing?

Cecilia brings forth a monstrous fish.

CECILIA: Listen to what the river is saying....

LIGHTS OUT.

THE END.

FOILS

The place: A town in Denmark.

We are in the shop of Sir Ulrich Fox, poisoners. It is a small and tidy place with one long counter and high shelves holding all the splendors and eruditions of the poisoner's art. There are some large colorful jars. A few small plants. A long sliding ladder. A few university diplomas and an exotic map of human anatomy upon the walls. There are numerous foils and fencing masks on display. It could be a florist shop or a fencing school, or a combination of the two. As the lights come up, we see Sir Ulrich Fox in a white apron dragging the body of one of his younger employees across the floor. The corpse is that of a young lad plainly dressed. There is a pork chop stuck in his teeth. Since motivation is the stuff of drama, Sir Ulrich's purpose is to dispose of the body in the alley behind his shop. Once that is accomplished, his life will return to normal. As he nears the end of the counter, we hear a bell tinkle. A door opens and Sir Ulrich's 19-year-old daughter enters. She is attractive, vivacious, and dressed as a splendid young woman of the 17th century might have dressed. She is in the eighth or ninth month of pregnancy.

ELMIRA: Father! What are you doing?
SIR ULRICH FOX: What does it look like I'm doing?
ELMIRA (*sarcastic*): Oh goody. A new game...I get to guess. Stop me if I'm wrong.
SIR ULRICH FOX: You're wrong.
ELMIRA (*removes her long white gloves*): Drag and carry, carry and drag. Dump the corpse in the alleyway...A game not quite as subtle as Twenty Questions, but I suppose it appeals to the lower classes. But then what doesn't these days–except opera.

Sir Ulrich drags the body offstage. We hear a door open, as the body is being dumped. The rear door slams shut, it locked. Sir Ulrich enters, rubbing his hands clean.

ELMIRA: You were experimenting with a new poison and you gave it to young Colin to test...

SIR ULRICH FOX: Wrong... if I were you, I would put those gloves back on.
ELMIRA: If I were you–is there a most useless phrase in the English language?
SIR ULRICH FOX: Button your lip. It was by far a better language before playwrights got hold of it.
ELMIRA (*pulling her gloves back on*): I suppose you want me to work this afternoon to fill in for young Colin.
SIR ULRICH FOX: Correct. I am expecting an important visitor...What with all that commotion up at the castle and all.
ELMIRA: Well, the Prince is mad, you know. Carrying on at *The Murder of Gonzago* the other night. All that leaping and lingering and placing his head in his girlfriend's lap.
SIR ULRICH FOX: I don't think she's his girlfriend.
ELMIRA: Oh, she is. Everybody knows it.
SIR ULRICH FOX: No. She's going to a nunnery.
ELMIRA: I don't believe it...She's bulimic. They don't allow all that throwing up in nunneries.....So what happened to your latest shop boy?
SIR ULRICH FOX: I told Colin to be careful.
ELMIRA: I'm sure you did.
SIR ULRICH FOX: I read him the riot act. Forbade him to linger among the belladonna. told him never to put his fingers to his mouth, insisted that if any customer requested *strychnia* that I, being an old hand at this profession, would fetch it....So what does the poor lout do?
ELMIRA (*moving some of the plants toward the window*): What does the poor lout do? Enquiring minds wish to know.
SIR ULRICH FOX: I brought him one of your mother's chops for lunch. I suggest he put some parsley on it. But he takes Fool's Parsley. He might as well have seasoned it with hemlock. Goes into convulsions just when I needed him to climb the ladder to fetch some Monkshood. And one. two, three, into convulsions he goes. Then stiff as a board. I couldn't even get the chop out from between his teeth....Shouldn't allow good meat to go to waste. Of course I would have the intelligence to wash the Fool's Parsley off it first.....Elmira, pass me the jar of Meadow–Saffron, please.
ELMIRA: I'm beginning to think you allow your assistants to work with you for a month and then you allow them to poison themselves so you won't have to pay them....Those are the rumors at any rate.

SIR ULRICH FOX: Rumors? Started by whom?
ELMIRA: By mother.
SIR ULRICH FOX: Of course, what else is marriage good for? Poisoning one's character. If you can't destroy one another physically, you can do it by innuendo....
ELMIRA: Well, if the mad prince marries the vomiting girl, it will be a marriage not made in heaven, I can tell you that. He's too intellectual and she hasn't got a serious bone in her body. It's obvious. The moment she stands up, you can see all her bones.
SIR ULRICH FOX: He should marry you, my dear....Especially in your present condition. What good is it to send a girl off to college if she comes home, not with her head-filled, but with her belly full? Hamlet must marry you.
ELMIRA: I don't believe I could stand all that upstairs/downstairs stuff.
SIR ULRICH FOX: What upstairs/downstairs stuff?
ELMIRA: Oh you know. Whatever you do in private upstairs somehow gets known to the servants downstairs and soon they're writing ballads and selling their memories to the highest bidder. In addition I don't think the Prince's mother would be a very nice woman to have for a mother-in-law.
SIR ULRICH FOX: I'm certain she has her virtues.
ELMIRA: She wouldn't know a virtue if the Pope carried one into her on a red velvet cushion...Imagine! Kissing her son full on the lips like that.
SIR ULRICH FOX: Oh the rich like that sort of thing, you know. Scandal is to royalty what skunk oil is to a fox hunt. It throws everybody off the scent.
ELMIRA: The scent of what?
SIR ULRICH FOX: Revolution. War. All the important things ideas that keep the peasants' noses pressed to the poisonous business of living. The present royal scandal makes it impossible to know what's going on with our war with Norway.
ELMIRA: Are we really at war?
SIR ULRICH FOX: In the presents state of affairs, it is difficult to tell. The King's personal life takes precedent over everything.
ELMIRA: That's why he keeps his mistresses close to home? Imagining bedding his brother's wife on the day of his brother's funeral!
SIR ULRICH FOX: I don't like talk of bedding in my shop.

ELMIRA: Of course not. But it's perfectly splendid of you to go around poisoning people.
SIR ULRICH FOX: I don't poison anyone. The study of lethal herbs, ungents, ointments, liqueurs, powders, etc. is my profession. And it is the highest of all professions. Knowing what can kill us is vital for the survival of our species..
ELMIRA: I, for one, shall not be relegated to a species, especially one addicted to such shallow amusements.
SIR ULRICH FOX: I supply people with what they need. I do not poison people!
ELMIRA: Then why is the alleyway behind our house is piled high with corpses?
SIR ULRICH FOX: Because we suffer from a slothful and desultory sanitation service. A more efficient Sanitation Department and our alleyways would sparkle.
ELMIRA: In your mind, disposing of corpses is next to Godliness...Excuse me while I take some of these Deadly Nightshade plants outside where our neighbors can toss their piss pots on them.

Elmira exits toward the rear of the store. As she exits, we hear the tinkling of the store's bell. The front door opens. Enter Voltimand, courier to the King.

SIR ULRICH FOX: Who's there? Stand and unfold yourself.
VOLTIMAND: Long live the king!
SIR ULRICH FOX: Voltimand?
VOLTIMAND: He....Formerly a she. But you know the benefits of science these days.
SIR ULRICH FOX: You come most carefully upon the hour.
VOLTIMAND: 'Tis now struck twelve.....Greetings from the king.

He strickes a low and obsequious bow.

SIR ULRICH FOX: Greetings from the King!..Oh my!
VOLTIMAND: From the soap opera at the top of the hill we call the castle.
SIR ULRICH FOX: It's a great honor.

VOLTIMAND: Yes, it is. King Claudius has requested me to inform you that he is planning a small soiree this weekend, and, as part of the festivities, there is going to be a display of fencing skills.
SIR ULRICH FOX: Fencing skills?
VOLTIMAND: A match if you will. Between the Prince, who is being billed as "The Melancholy Dane"–a real crowd-pleaser that moniker–and the son of the late Polonius–Laertes "The Terminator Late From Paris"... as soon as the match was announced, the event was sold out. Standing Room only.
SIR ULRICH FOX: Does the King desire a new set of foils?
VOLTIMAND: No. We're up to our neck in foils. What we need is something to put on the tip of the foils, something....well I don't know how to put it delicately...
SIR ULRICH FOX: Poisonous.
VOLTIMAND: That's delicate enough. Very poisonous, in fact. Yes, the King said you are good at that sort of thing.
SIR ULRICH FOX: Please tell His Highness that I am honored to be in his good graces.

Sir Ulrich Fox climbs the ladder to fetch some poisons.

SIR ULRICH FOX: Something to put on the tip of a sword, you say?
VOLTIMAND (*opening a piece of parchment and studying it*): And something that will dissolve readily in a cup of wine.
SIR ULRICH FOX: Red or white?
VOLTIMAND: Doesn't say. Or if does say, I can't read the writing. It is certain to be a cheap wine imported from some region that has never heard of grapes.

He passes the slip of royal parchment to Sir Ulrich to read. Elmira enters carrying an apron.

ELMIRA: It's one thing to toss out the assistant, but it's quite another to waste good aprons. I was going to pull Colin's trousers off, but the neighbors would have gotten the wrong idea, one more misconception to add to their stockpile of venomous gossip.
SIR ULRICH FOX: Neighbors are nearby folk who possess all the wrong ideas.

VOLTIMAND: And who is this enchanting species?
ELMIRA: When did I become a species all of a sudden?
VOLTIMAND (*bows*): Forgive me. You are one of a kind.
SIR ULRICH FOX: Speaking, as she was, of misconceptions, allow me to present my daughter Elmira. She, like your Prince, is home from Wittenberg where she had been studying Medicine...and, I hesitate to add, anatomy... Daughter, this Voltimand, Courier to the King.
ELMIRA: I believe I glimpsed you at *The Murder of Gonzago* the other evening. Did you enjoy the play?
VOLTIMAND: It demanded more music, don't you think?
ELMIRA: I can't think of anything in life that would not benefit from more music.
SIR ULRICH FOX (*to his daughter*): Except The Wedding March....The king is need of our services.
ELMIRA (*Curtseys)*: We are here to serve.
SIR ULRICH FOX (*to his daughter)*: He can see that already.

Sir Ulrich Fox climbs the ladder and hands down to his daughter several jars.

SIR ULRICH FOX: Now the question before us is: Do you believe the king would prefer a Corrosive Poison, an Irritant poison, or a systemic Poison? Do you have any opinions on the subject?
VOLTIMAND: I know nothing about your profession.
SIR ULRICH FOX: Nonsense. Everyone is an expert on poisoning. It's the essence of being human.
ELMIRA: Especially poisoning relationships....Is there any Purple Foxglove left?
VOLTIMAND: An irritant poisoning sounds too lightweight. The King wishes to do much more than irritate his victim.
SIR ULRICH FOX: All three types are very effective, but they work differently. Corrosive poisons destroy living tissues. Irritants inflame the mucous membranes by attacking them directly. Systemic poisons attack the victim's nervous system.
VOLTIMAND: Attacking the nervous system. I like that.
ELMIRA: Is that what the King prefers?

VOLTIMAND: The King demands that the poison be fast-working. He doesn't want to sit about waiting for his victim to die. That would prove embarrassing.
SIR ULRICH FOX: We understand.
ELMIRA: Waiting around for people to die is always so annoying.
SIR ULRICH FOX: It seems to be the essence of family relationships....
ELMIRA: What do we have on hand that could prove useful? (*Reads labels on the jars.)* Laudanum. Cyanide....
SIR ULRICH FOX (*holds out a jar)*: Smell! ..It smells like bitter almonds.
ELMIRA: Then there's Belladonna which could give the victim a rash that resembles Scarlet fever....See how pretty it is. I'll spread some on the back of my glove. Nearly invisible.

She shows him crushed belladonna leaves on the back of her glove.

SIR ULRICH FOX (*holds out another jar)*: Which raises the question of whether the King wishes to have the act of poisoning remain undetected.
VOLTIMAND: That is preferable, isn't it?
SIR ULRICH FOX: What is preferable is not always possible. The more effective poisons all have their tell-tale traces. *Strychnia* is good. Causes spasmodic contractions of the muscles. The body of your victim becomes stiff as a board. But the eyeballs will bulge out fairly prominently, which might give the game away.
ELMIRA: Much of the effect of any poison depends upon how that poison is administered. Do we know how the king is going to use our powders? Will he pour it into the ear while his victim is sleeping?
SIR ULRICH FOX: One poison is to be applied to the tip of a sword blade while the other is to be dissolved in a cheap Siberian wine.
ELMIRA: We could give you *Nux Vomica* in the form of a powder. You could make a paste of it. Then apply it to the tip of the foil....You can see that it is nearly invisible. I spread on the back of my glove and you can't see it...(*She spreads some on the back of her glove and holds it forth for Voltimand to examine.)* See?
VOLTIMAND: Splendid...But the King would prefer that the victim die quickly and in great pain. The body should be wracked with seizures. Eyes might roll back into the skull.

SIR ULRICH FOX: Poor Laertes.
VOLTIMAND: Not poor Laertes...Poor Hamlet, I should say. ..
ELMIRA (*gasps, puts her hand over her heart*): Hamlet?...Did you say Hamlet?
VOLTIMAND: Oh, maybe I'm speaking out of turn, but Claudius indicated you could be trusted.
ELMIRA: But Hamlet's his own nephew...Stepson...
VOLTIMAND: I can't understand my own family, let alone someone else's.
ELMIRA: You must have misunderstood.
VOLTIMAND: I believe it is you who misunderstand. Claudius hates his stepson. His mother should never have sent him off to college. Educating Royalty is like adding sauce to caviar. It's so unnecessary. They're only taking up space that should go to a student who really needs it. A Prince already has his profession.. Being the Prince is a profession.

Elmira goes behind the counter to wrap the small packages of poison.

SIR ULRICH FOX: The King hates Hamlet. Hamlet hates the King. The People hate the king. Laertes hates Hamlet. Christians hate non-Christians. Upper classes hate the lower classes. Strangers hate strangers. We hate anyone who is not like ourselves .And you say you know nothing about poisons. God poisoned the wells before we even took our first drink. Poison flows through the universe and humans are merely the conduits.
VOLTIMAND (*a rhetorical question*): You enjoy your profession, don't you?
SIR ULRICH FOX: It's an important one. And it has its moments of ecstatic discovery. Such as when one sees for the first time some bark from the Ordeal Tree in Africa...or stumbles upon Deadly Nightshade growing in the wild. The irony of it all is how beautiful some of the poisons are. Takes the breath away....figuratively and literally.
ELMIRA (Brings forth two packages wrapped in plain brown paper and tied with string): Here are the poisons you request...The first is for the Fencing Match. As soon as the victim's skin is pierced, he will stop in his tracks. His chest will contract. It will appear as if the victim has died from suffocation. Unable to catch his breath.

VOLTIMAND: Excellent. But one point to be observed. There is to be no vomiting involved. The Queen has put down a new carpet for the occasion, and watching guests vomit all over it will put the royal household in a snit. And you don't want to be there when the royal household is in a snit.
SIR ULRICH FOX: I doubt if we can control the vomiting of the guests. The behaviour of theatre audiences is beyond human understanding.
VOLTIMAND: I meant the victim.
SIR ULRICH FOX: He won't have to time to vomit. He goes out in a flash.
ELIMIRA: This second package is for the wine. Since it will be an inferior wine, chosen for an inferior occasion, I doubt if the poison will at all affect the taste. Two or three sips should do the trick, I should think. I've written the King's name on the packets.
VOLTIMAND: I am amazed that such a pretty head should contain such diabolical secrets.
ELMIRA: Don't get the two packages confused.
VOLTIMAND: I am certain that King Claudius shall amply reward you for your efforts. The party will be a stunning success.
SIR ULRICH FOX: Some reforms in the Sanitation Department might be entertained.

Voltimand takes up one of Elmira's gloved hands.

VOLTIMAND: I trust we shall meet again. When you are in a more sporting condition.
ELMIRA: Oh, I am in a sporting condition now.
VOLTIMAND: When is the bastard due?
ELMIRA: Any moment.

Voltimand starts out, but before he reaches the door, he grabs his throat and his eyes bulge. He suffers convulsions.

VOLTIMAND: What's happening to me?

Voltimand falls to the floor dead.

SIR ULRICH FOX (*to Elmira*): I knew you were up to something.
ELMIRA: He kissed the glove that had the *nux vomica* on it.
SIR ULRICH FOX: I have never approved of hand kissing.
ELMIRA: Voltimand enjoyed it far less than you.
SIR ULRICH FOX: But I'm the one who has to drag and carry. Drag and Carry.
ELMIRA (*removing her gloves*): I can't let them poison my Hamlet.

Sir Ulrich Fox prepares to drag Voltimand away.

ELMIRA: I'll take the packages up to the castle, bring them directly to Hamlet, and tell him of the plot. We'll see whose foil gets the poison.
SIR ULRICH FOX: I'm certain it's all going to work out the way you wish.
ELMIRA: Tell mother not to wait up for me. It could be a long evening of plotting and counterplotting.
SIR ULRICH FOX: Well, the Prince has a head for that sort of thing. His uncle, too.

Elmira takes her packages and exits. Sir Ulrich drags Voltimand to the alley.

SIR ULRICH FOX: Ah, Voltimand. Why do you weigh so much? If I were King. Ah, are there any more useless words in all the language? If I were King, my courtiers would be, light weight dwarves, midgets. In order to get rid of a corpse, especially a corpse not of one's own making, a man should not have to throw his back out.

We hear a door open, a body being dumped. The rear door slams shut and is locked. Sir Ulrich enters rubbing his hands clean. He starts up the ladder.

SIR ULRICH FOX: It's getting far too crowded out there. What I should do is go into another, less messy profession. Extracting teeth? But that's too painful, both for the patient and the doctor. Besides, I was meant for this profession. Ever since I was a small boy, I have been enamored of rare and exotic plants. To me the Deadly Nightshade is more beautiful than a rose. Well, I guess I better climb the ladder and put these jars back before closing.

A bell tingles. The front door opens. A middle-aged peasant woman enters.

WOMAN: Sir Ulrich? Sir Ulrich! Come quick!
SIR ULRICH FOX: What is it?
WOMAN: Your daughter. Her water broke. She's going to give birth!
SIR ULRICH FOX (*scurries down the ladder*): Where?
WOMAN: In front of The Coffined Aria. We carried her inside.
SIR ULRTCH FOX (*untying his apron*): But her packages?
WOMAN: And don't stir your head with that nonsense. You have more important matters to think about. I had my eldest take the packages for you. King Claudius will get them. Don't you worry.
SIR ULRICH FOX: King Claudius?
WOMAN: Yes. Thank God my son spotted the name on the packets. He's on his way to the castle even as I speak
SIR ULRICH FOX: But but but...
WOMAN (*grabs him by the hand*): But nothing. You're going to be a grandfather. The king gets what he ordered. Your daughter gets what you ordered. All's right with the world. Soon you will have new life to celebrate. What can be more important than that?

They go out. The small bell rings.

LIGHTS OUT.

END OF PLAY.

TRAGEDY: A COMEDY

Time: The recent present. The curtain opens upon a simple classroom scene: a blackboard, a desk, a few chairs for the pupils. There is, in fact, only one student–David Nims, a young man of 19 or so. Eager. The professor, on the other hand, Dr. Amos Whitestone, nearing seventy and running out of things to say–appears to be more eager/nervous than his student. Dressed in a tweedy suit, he takes his place at the front of the class, blows the dust off his notes, and opens his roll book. He then crosses to the door, looks out, peers down a hallway we do not see, then shuts the door and returns to his desk.

DR. AMOS WHITESTONE: Well, class how good to see everyone here.

DAVID NIMS looks about the classroom. He is puzzled.

DR. AMOS WHITESTONE: To get us started. I'll call the roll. If I mispronounce your name, please correct me...Gently..I'll go through the list quickly...David Nims.
DAVID NIMS: Here!
DR. AMOS WHITESTONE: Done....I'm glad you received my postcard about the room change.

He closes his roll book.

DR. AMOS WHITESTONE: Now, many students who have signed up for my course–THE HISTORY OF COMEDY–are under the false impression that it's going to be fun and games. A laugh a minute. So I wish to correct that false impression immediately. There's nothing funny about this course. There's nothing funny about comedy per se. Indeed, if I hear any inappropriate laughter, giggling, guffaws–out you go. (SLAMS A STRAIGHT EDGE ON THE DESK). Damn. This is the most serious course this university offers. Comedy is not a laughing matter and every one of you had better get it through your heads at once.

David Nims has been waving his hand in the air.

DR. AMOS WHITESTONE: Yes....Mr...Mr... *(He opens his roll book.)*
DAVID NIMS: David Nims...I am David Nims.
DR. AMOS WHITESTONE: Ah, so you are....You have a question for me, Mr. Nims? I marked you present if that's what you're worried about.
DAVID NIMS: I'm just curious. Am I the only one who signed up for this course?
DR. AMOS WHITESTONE: I am curious too. What does it matter how many sign up for Comedy? If you wish to learn the contents of the course, I am here to teach it. Every Monday, Wednesday, and Friday at he ungodly hour of 8 A.M. when the only sound of laughter that can be heard is from the infernal milkman upbraiding his horse for being too slow. Those milk bottles clanging away. bringing poison into every household, signaling the dawn of a new day of desperation.
DAVID NIMS: What I mean to say, sir, is...well, will the administration run a course with only one student in it?

Dr. Amos Whitestone reopens his roll book and studies the single name entered therein.

DR. AMOS WHITESTONE: I have been a member of the staff...if staff is the appropriate word.....for decades now. I am encrusted, as it were...like a barnacle...so there are prerogatives to be enjoyed. We shall run the run the course to its bitter end. Does that make you happier, Mr. Nims?
DAVID NIMS *(uncertain):* Thank you, Sir.
DR. AMOS WHITESTONE: Oh, don't thank me. It's merely the inertia of administration. They don't know what to do with me, and I don't know what to do with them....Now, allow us to begin our exploration of comedy... The first text is *Hamlet* by William Shakespeare...I hope you brought the book to class.

David Nims holds up his edition of Hamlet.

DR. AMOS WHITESTONE: Good. I can see we're going to get along fine.
DAVID NIMS: Dr. Whitestone?
DR. AMOS WHITESTONE: Yes, Mr. Nims?

DAVID NIMS: Isn't *Hamlet* a tragedy?
DR. AMOS WHITESTONE (*his edition is held together by rubber bands and tape*): I don't see how it could be.
DAVID NIMS: Almost everybody refers to it as a tragedy....even on the title page it says "The Tragedy of Hamlet, Prince of Denmark"
DR. AMOS WHITESTONE: You can't believe everything you read. I hope you've learned that lesson by now.
DAVID NIMS: Yes, sir.
DR. AMOS WHITESTONE: I don't see how it's possible in a story where a young man (say around forty) finally returns home from college, spies a white rabbit running across the castle grounds, chases said rabbit, and falls down a rabbit hole and meets an assortment of weirdos, including Rosencrantz and Guildenstern who recite a poem about a rattle....How could any critic hold that story to be a tragedy? I mean isn't it obvious that it is absolutely hilarious when Hamlet and Ophelia play croquet using flamingos as mallets?
DAVID NIMS: Well, that would be hilarious...
DR. AMOS WHITESTONE: Of course. So take your pen and cross out the word tragedy and write in comedy.

Dr. Whitestone crosses to the door, opens the door, peers down a corridor we cannot see, shuts the door, returns to his podium.

DAVID NIMS: Professor?
DR. AMOS WHITESTONE: Go ahead. Do it. I can't understand persons who are reluctant to write in books.
DAVID NIMS: Is your *Hamlet* is the same as my *Hamlet*?
DR. AMOS WHITESTONE: I don't know. I think that is a question for philosophers to decide. Did you purchase the Aukland Edition as I recommended?
DAVID NIMS: Well, I had an edition left over from high school...
DR. AMOS WHITESTONE: Well, there you are. There is a big difference between *Hamlet* in high school and *Hamlet* in college. I mean, many local schools censor the scene where Hamlet grows to be fifteen feet high and then encounters Ophelia at a tea party. That's why it's important to get the right edition...The one listed on the syllabus. The Aukland edition. It carries an excellent introduction....written by myself, actually.

DAVID NIMS: You mean that Shakespeare wrote another play called *Hamlet,* where Hamlet doesn't die at the end?
DR. AMOS WHITESTONE: Of course Hamlet dies at the end. Don't you remember? He's playing croquet with Ophelia, and the queen–his mother–accidentally hits him in the head with a croquet ball. Hamlet falls to the ground and cries out.... "It's a far far better thing I do than I have ever done before."

David Nims leafs frantically through Hamlet, trying to locate the pertinent scene.

DAVID NIMS: I can't find that scene.
DR. AMOS WHITESTONE: Of course you can't find it. You don't have the Aukland edition.
DAVID NIMS: I'm sorry. I'll buy it right after class.
DR. AMOS WHITESTONE: Forget it..Take mine... I remember what it's like to be an undergraduate and to be penniless, always at the mercy of the elements...All 118 of them...Or however many elements there are. Starting with hydrogen...ending with transistors.
DAVID NIMS: Thank you....But, professor, may I ask a question?
DR. AMOS WHITESTONE: Naturally. Questions are at the heart of the educational process. Tuition first, questions second....you have paid your tuition, haven't you? I hate it when the bursar pulls a student out of my class for nonpayment of tuition...and just when we're getting off to a fast start.
DAVID NIMS: I've paid.
DR. AMOS WHITESTONE: Good. That's my question. What's your question...and please don't say "To be or not to be, that is the question. " I am so tired of that sophomoric joke. Sophomores are so...sophomoric, aren't they? What year are you in, Mr. Nims?
DAVID NIMS: Third year. But I am a transfer student.
DR. AMOS WHITESTONE: Good. I am a transfer teacher. What I know I try to transfer to another person's petrified brains.
DAVID NIMS: If Hamlet dies at the end....especially if he's killed by his mother by a croquet ball....Can we rightly say the play is a comedy? Doesn't death at the end of a play mean a tragedy?
DR. AMOS WHITESTONE: Good point, Mr. Nims..good point. I can see we're going to have many a lively discussion....Where can I begin?

You are familiar with the classical definition of comedy? Comedy traditionally ends with a marriage.
DAVID NIMS: Yes. You wrote that in the catalogue description.
DR. AMOS WHITESTONE: I did?
DAVID NIMS: You taped it to your postcard.
DR. AMOS WHITESTONE: I did? I seem to be getting more efficient every year. Youth has so much more energy to waste; hence, comedy. Old age, on the other crutch, has to be efficient to a fare-thee-well. Hence, Tragedy....What does my catalogue description say?
DAVID NIMS *(reads):* It says: THE HISTORY OF COMEDY, Monday, Wednesday, Friday, 8AM to 9:00. Professor Amos Whitehead. Required texts: *Hamlet* by William Shakespeare, *The Tibetan Book of the Dead,* Sigmund Freud's *Jokes and Their Relation to the Unconscious,* and Plato's *Symposium*.. Comedy traditionally ends with marriage; tragedy ends with death. Students will be required to do one or the other..." Professor, maybe that's why students aren't signing up. Isn't your reading list is pretty heavy for a course about comedy?
DR. AMOS WHITESTONE: I probably should bring the catalogue description up to date. A lot has changed since I first wrote that description.
DAVID NIMS: Such as?
DR. AMOS WHITESTONE: The Atom bomb. The hydrogen bomb. Ethnic cleansing. the Holocaust....The world isn't such a funny place anymore. In the face of such harsh conditions, students would rather look at movies....Who can blame them? Look at this article that I clipped out of the newspaper some time ago. (*He takes out a yellowed newspaper clipping and reads it).* "The world's oldest known captive goldfish has died at the age of (at least 43). The goldfish was won by seven year old Peter Hand at a fairground and it outlived all of Hand's other pets. When Peter grew up he moved in with his parents and brought the goldfish with him. Last year, the goldfish–named Tish–acquired a distinguished silver color and was recognized by the Guinness Book of Records as the world's oldest captive goldfish. Hilda Hand found him dead at the bottom of his fish tank. I am very sad...Over the years we have become very close and I could sense if he was happy or not."...So now class, tell me. Is that comedy or tragedy?
DAVID NIMS: People are sad over its death.

DR. AMOS WHITESTONE: It's only a goldfish....I've seen that more than once. People who wax sentimental over the death of pets don't think twice about putting their enemies to death. Hitler probably wept at the death of puppies.

DAVID NIMS: How can you say it's only a goldfish? It was created by God. All living things are sacred.

DR. AMOS WHITESTONE: Don't drag God into it. God doesn't have a sense of humor, or He wouldn't have invented yoghurt. Yoghurt everybody has to take seriously. Tragedy or comedy, Mr. Nims?

DAVID NIMS: You are setting me up with a false dilemma.

DR. AMOS WHITESTONE: *False dilemma*? I haven't heard that phrase since my marriage ceremony....You are religious and philosophical all together.

DAVID NIMS: Who isn't?

DR. AMOS WHITETONE: Goldfish. Especially ones that are over forty years old...It was probably senile, swimming round and round, thinking to itself: " When are they going to change the water in this bowl? And can't I ever get something good to eat, like ham and eggs? Sure my owners think I am only a goldfish, but in another life I was a philosopher named Socrates. My being has only been recycled into a lower form. But still I have my pride. I also have $73,000 in retirement funds socked away under the plastic model of a pirate ship in the corner of this tank."

DAVID NIMS: Are you talking about reincarnation, Professor?

DR. AMOS WHITESTONE: No, I am talking about retirement...
Investing for the future....Look, my dear student, many many persons believe in reincarnation. And if reincarnation is a fact, Mr. Nims, then Tragedy with a capital T is a fraud. There is no end to life. Every one knows that. Our cells are merely recycled. Matter cannot be created nor destroyed. So where is the Tragedy. It melts together–the comic and tragic. We laugh through our tears to keep from killing ourselves. Is that not true?

DAVID NIMS: I am supposed to learn all this from the death of a goldfish?

DR. AMOS WHITESTONE: Every year I ask the same questions. I merely change the answers. It's called the Socratic method...Do you know what the Socratic method of teaching is, Mr. Nims?

DAVID NIMS: Is that where you ask me a question such as "What is justice?" and I then I give an answer and you make a fool of me?
DR. AMOS WHITESTONE: You're much too sensitive, Mr. Nims. The universe makes fools of us all. It wasn't the Big Bang that brought the planets into being, it was God's sardonic laughter...A cosmic belch. Perhaps it would help if I showed you Walt Disney's version of *Plato's Symposium,* The scene I emphasize in class is where Agathon and Socrates get into a debate about which is better Comedy or Tragedy....In the animated film they are played by Mickey and Clarabelle...I forget who plays whom. Anyway, after singing a bouncy little song called " We Whistle a Happy Epistemology," Clarabelle insists that the Muse of Comedy is the same as the Muse of Tragedy. Agathon, of course, has won the prize for tragedy and has celebrated with an all-night drinking party, a symposium if you will. I quote from the ancient text: "Aristodemus did not hear the beginning of the discourse, and he was only half awake, but the chief thing which he remembered, was Socrates insisting to the other two that the genius of comedy was the same as that of tragedy, and that the writer of tragedy ought to be a writer of comedy also. To this they were compelled to assent, being sleepy, and not quite understanding his meaning."
DAVID NIMS (*returns to the catalogue description of the course*): The description in the catalogue says that you are going to bring in guest speakers...
DR. AMOS WHITESTONE: Ah, I see that Mr. Nims did not hear the beginning of my discourse either....being sleepy and not quite understanding my meaning.
DAVID NIMS: It says you bring in a mime and a comedian named Buckminster Fuller.
DR. AMOS WHITESTONE: Well, not a comedian exactly. A philosopher and an inventor. A pretty funny man. though. He wrote a book that he was hoping to sell to Hollywood. It was called "A Tree Grows in the Head of Movie Producers." But the best-laid plans of mice and men don't always work out. Hence, the comic imagination.
DAVID NIMS: But isn't Buckminster Fuller dead?
DR. AMOS WHITESTONE: Well, I told you the catalogue copy is a bit out of date, didn't I?
DAVID NIMS (*sorely disappointed*): So I'm stuck with the mime?

DR. AMOS WHITESTONE: Sorry, Mr. Nims. No mime this semester. The last time I brought a mime to class all he did was try to walk against a strong wind. I couldn't stand it. So I broke his legs....A very unhappy experience for all concerned.
DAVID NIMS: You broke his legs?
DR. AMOS WHITESTONE: Not exactly on purpose. I playfully whacked him across the knees with a lead pipe....Discipline, Mr. Nims...Discipline. It's the heart of comedy. It may look like anarchy, but anarchy leads to tragedy...Classical comedy, on the other hand, leads to what?
DAVID NIMS: To marriage.
DR. AMOS WHITESTONE: And which is worse, Mr. Nims, death or marriage?
DAVID NIMS: I'm not certain, sir. I've never been married.
DR. AMOS WHITESTONE: Then I'll tell you the answer. From experience. I have been married. To a woman who preferred cosmetics to Tacitus... Our honeymoon was studded with phrases such as "False Dilemma" and " Max Factor." And so, I tell you, my young friend, that marriage is much worse than death. Thus, the endings to comedies are much more brutal than the endings to tragedies. Mark my words. You'll find out some day. Do you have a girlfriend?
DAVID NIMS: No. I'm saving my money to buy a motorcycle.
DR. AMOS WHITESTONE *(pulling pages from a three-ringed notebook, he holds up one page)*: Shall we get serious, Mr. Nims? Let's look for a moment at one of the fundamental ideas behind Shakespearean comedy. The scholar William E. Slights, writing for the *University of Toronto Quarterly*, tells us that "...much of Shakespearean comedy deals with the execution of justice. Meting out measure for measure, punishing a usurer, or forgiving a Wicked Brother provides comic reversals, liberation from ritual bondage, and a hopeful communal future..." I don't see you taking notes on any of this, Mr. Nims.
DAVID NIMS: My pen has run out of ink.
DR. AMOS WHITESTONE: Good planning, Mr. Nims.. good planning. I ask you to cross out one word, change tragedy to comedy, and there you are, left in the backwater of scholarly illumination...You have five dollars? You can buy my pen....
DAVID NIMS: Five dollars?

DR. AMOS WHITESTONE: Just kidding, Mr. Nims....Just kidding. Don't you have a sense of humor?...Here, take my pen...Take everything from me...Everybody else has! Rush into my classroom without a working pen, drain me of all my ideas, and leave me a hollow shell, not fit for anything but some looney bin! Vultures! You are all nothing but vultures. Stealing a man's soul for a few sordid academic credits. Vultures! You are all nothing but vultures. Stealing a man's soul for a few sordid academic credits.
DAVID NIMS: Professor! Are you all right?
DR. AMOS WHITESTONE: Sorry...Where were we?
DAVID NIMS: You were selling me your pen.
DR. AMOS WHITESTONE: Before that.
DAVID NIMS: Something about comedy and the sense of justice.
DR. AMOS WHITESTONE: If comedy ends with a hopeful communal future, what does tragedy end with?
DAVID NIMS: Death?
DR. AMOS WHITESTONE: No...No...No. Violent death. Death is nothing, my young friend...why, look at this jar of sleeping pills I have with me. I'll just swallow the entire bottle and exit this world...Just to prove to you that death is nothing....A mere bagatelle for poets, dramatists, and kamikaze pilots...(*lifts the bottle to his lips. Nims leaps from his chair and knocks the bottle of pills to the floor.)*
DAVID NIMS: Professor, what's wrong with you?
DR. WHITESTONE: You haven't heard of audio-visual aids?....I'm giving you a lesson you'll never forget....Now sit down and take notes...unless you've already ruined my 100 year old pen, a family heirloom....
DAVID NIMS: You frightened me.
DR. WHITESTONE (*collecting the spilled pills):* If I couldn't frighten students, I would quit teaching in two minutes....Power! That's what teachers want...Power ..I want to see students reduced to gibbering gerbils...panicked animals rolling about on the floor, pleading for mercy.
DAVID NIMS (*stands up*): I think I'm going to be late for my next class...
DR. WHITESTONE: Sit down!

David Nims does as he is told.

DR. WHITESTONE: You see, Mr. Nims, tragedy can be avoided...as you so superbly demonstrated by knocking the lethal medicine from my hands...If it couldn't be avoided, it wouldn't be tragedy...All Lear had to say was "Cordelia, I love you anyway. Forget my silly game and claim your dowry..." Critics will tell you that once the process starts everything that follows is inevitable...Of course, it is inevitable, but the marble that puts the game into play never should have been played in the first place. With tragedy, you go over and over in your head all the permutations of time...If I had done this and not that...If she had taken a later flight...If I had decided to stay home from work that day...or as A.E. Housman said it so much better than my humble self: "Oh, at home had I but stayed/Prenticed to my father's trade/Had I stuck to plane and adze./I had not been lost my lads." No. It's comedy that cannot be avoided. You're going to get the pie in the face, no matter which way you turn, because God is an expert pie thrower. ..Job cries out from his ash-heap, "Not the cream-pie, O Lord....Hit me with the lemon-meringue.." That's the revised standard, of course. It's slightly more elegant in the King James' version ...Not much laughter in the *Bible*.. Christ never laughed. But that will be the subject of our next lesson. That, and the Old Testament: "Hath thou given the horse thunder; has thou peed in the pockets of the depraved. Hath thou pitched a tent in the head of ithe Father who has lost his son?" ...Now, let's consider the theories of that master jokesmith Sigmund Freud....

DAVID NIMS (*madly taking notes*): Is all of this going to be on the final?

DR. WHITESTONE: All of this and more.... there is only one question in the all the universe worth asking, and it is: "Is this going to be on the final?" Yes, Sigmund Freud's *Jokes and Their Relation to the Unconscious* will be on the final...I didn't want to scare too many students away....But don't panic, Mr. Nims. I'll give you the answer.

DAVID NIMS: To what question?

DR. WHITESTONE: "Why is a raven like a writing desk?" "Because Poe wrote on both of them!" ...Forget the question. Concentrate on the answer. The answer is "Eifersucht is a Leidenschaft which mit Eifer sucht what Leiden schafft." Get it?

DAVID NIMS: How do you spell *Leidenschaft*?

DR. WHITESTONE: You don't know German?

DAVID NIMS: Oh, I come from a very academic family. I had a year of scientific German. If you stick to oxygen and other burning stuff, I might be able to follow a couple of sentences, spoken slowly...with simultaneous translation.
DR. WHITESTONE: Education is not what it used to be. In my day we had to study German. Just in case we were overcome with a sudden desire to conquer the world.
DAVID NIMS: At my school you could take either two years of language or one year of scientific German and a second year of editing video tape.
DR. AMOS WHITESTONE: Video tape editing? Very well, I'll translate for you. Eifersucht (jealousy) is a Leidenschaft (passion) which mit Eifer sucht (with eagerness seeks) what Leiden schafft (causes pain). That's the answer.
DAVID NIMS: What's the question again?
DR. AMOS WHITESTONE: Doesn't Sigmund Freud have a sense of humor? Obviously not. His book is riddled with the worst examples of jokes in the history of the world. (*Leafs through his notes*). Here's another one: "And, as true as God shall grant me all good things, Doctor, I sat beside Salommon Rothschild and he treated me quite as his equal–quite famillionairely." Here, I'll write the pun on the board so you can see what so amused the Father of Psychiatry.

Dr. Whitestone writes famillionairely on the chalk board.

DR. AMOS WHITESTONE (underlines *millionairely*): Then Freud goes on to say that "Heymans and Lipps used this joke (which is admittedly an excellent and most amusing one)." If that joke is an excellent and amusing one, I am a horse's patootie....Of course, if you can charge people $250 an hour to talk to you about their most intimate feelings, you can afford to find anything funny....
DAVID NIMS: I don't believe Freud charged $250 an hour.
DR. AMOS WHITEHEAD: What do you know about inflation in Vienna?
DAVID NIMS (*humbled*): Nothing... *(changing the subject)* So Freud isn't funny, but *Hamlet* is...

Dr. Whitestone writes comedy and tragedy on the chalk board.

DR. AMOS WHITESTONE: Now we're getting somewhere.... Sigmund Freud's *Jokes and Their Relation to the Unconscious*–if you can find one funny joke in it, I'll eat it....I'll tear a page out of the text, salt and pepper it, and devour it like a bon bon....(*demonstrates*). Yum...That's the final examination question: try to find something funny that violates the saying "Eifersucht is a Leidenschaft which mit Eifer sucht what Leiden schafft." My pain is tragedy. Your pain borders on the comic....But comedy is fleeting. Comedy is time-bound. Contemporary. Up to the minute. Aristophanes' jokes about eels from Boetia don't stand up. Reading *The Clouds*, where a father and son are separated by philosophy, you would have to spend half your days in the footnotes. (*mumbles*) Father and son.

The door flies open and in rushes the dean of the college accompanied by a security guard.

DEAN OF THE COLLEGE: That's him....Arrest him.
SECURITY GUARD (*raises his night stick*): You're not going to give me any trouble this year, are you, Dr. Whitestone?
DAVID NIMS: Is this part of the humor? Am I suppose to take notes on this?
DR. AMOS WHITESTONE (*closing his notebook. He circles the room to avoid capture):* When did I give anyone any trouble?
DEAN OF THE COLLEGE: When did you give anyone any trouble? That's the funniest line I've heard all day...
DR. AMOS WHITESTONE: Write that down, Mr. Nims...It might be useful on the final...
DAVID NIMS: What did the professor do? He was just teaching his class...
DEAN OF THE COLLEGE: And who are you?
DAVID NIMS: I'm David Nims...I'm enrolled in this course --The History of Comedy...Monday, Wednesday, and Friday...
SECURITY GUARD *(gently):* Come along, Professor...I'll take you back to the home...
DAVID NIMS: Professor, this is your pen, I believe.
DR. AMOS WHITESTONE: Keep it...a souvenir...Something to remember me by...A gift.
DAVID NIMS: I'm sorry I dropped it.

DR. AMOS WHITESTONE: Good day, Mr, Nims. It was a pleasure having you in my class. I have every confidence you shall do well...After all, it isn't brain surgery. It could have been brain surgery if I had a scapel instead of a pen.

Dr. Whitestone is led from the classroom. The door is closed.

DAVID NIMS: What happened?
DEAN OF THE COLLEGE: Mr. Nims, you deserve an explanation...
DAVID NIMS: Who are you?
DEAN OF THE COLLEGE: I am Wesker Nexberry, Dean of the College. First, I wish to apologize to you for all of the confusion...You see this is not the first time this little mix-up has happened...This educational fiasco...Where do I begin?
DAVID NIMS: You cancelled the class because not enough students signed up for it?
DEAN OF THE COLLEGE: No. The History of Comedy is being taught...By Professor Waxman in another building. You should be in Professor Waxman's class...Not here.
DAVID NIMS: But I got this postcard from Dr. Whitestone announcing a room change.
DEAN OF THE COLLEGE: Yes, yes...I am not surprised. He's done that sort of thing before. Finds the name of one of the students, gets hold of a empty classroom, sends out a postcard, and lures the hapless student into his den.
DAVID NIMS: For what purpose? To harm me? The old man didn't come near me.
DEAN OF THE COLLEGE: No. For the most pathetic reason of all. To go on teaching.
DAVID NIMS: You mean he wants to teach the course in Comedy and our college won't let him?
DEAN OF THE COLLEGE: Oh he's not a teacher. He was a milkman. Delivered milk every day to the college faculty and students....Mr. Nims, what I am going to you must be held in strictest confidence. I don't want to have this scandal bandied about.
DAVID NIMS: I won't bandy.
DEAN OF THE COLLEGE: Then by being around the University so long he got it into his head that he wanted to teach a course in Tragedy.

He delivered milk in the morning, went to classes in the afternoon. But then it came to light that Amos Whitestone was doing more than delivering milk to the apartment of the President. He was having an affair with wife of the president of the college. Many people thought it was suspicious to see a milkman delivering fresh cream at eleven in the morning. But, one thing led to another, and the two of them ran off together --I mean the president's wife and the milkman scholar. The president was distraught and attempted to commit suicide. The wife, feeling guilty over her lack of morals and becoming tired of getting up every morning at 3 A.M. to help deliver milk, left her lover and returned home.. Unfortunately, she was pregnant with Whitestone's child. Her husband agreed to raise the child, provided of course that the child–born a boy–would never see or come contact with Whitestone. This condition was rigorously adhered to.

DAVID NIMS: How long ago did this happen?

DEAN OF STUDENTS: I would say about nineteen or twenty years ago. The boy would be about your age, I should think. That was when Whitestone decided to throw up the milk business and become a scholar. He took classes and earned his doctorate in literature, with now a new emphasis on theories of comedy....

DAVID NIMS: I thought he was very good...

DEAN OF THE COLLEGE: I am sure he has one good lecture in him....Most people do. He did his dissertation on "The Comic Motives in *Hamlet*" and graduated with honors. But still his heart was broken. He had only one goal in life–to return to this college in triumph. To deliver brilliant lectures here and win back his beloved Elizabeth. But, of course, there was no way that he was going to be allowed to step one milkman foot on this campus ever again. He could have taught in other schools, but he turned all other offers down. He tried to deliver some lectures on *Alice In Wonderland* in town, but nobody came...He was *persona non grata* in this community, I can tell you that. No one was interested in anything that seducer had to say. Since no one wanted to hear what he had to say, Dr. Whitestone took it his head to give up speaking. He became, for a short time, one of those pathetic mimes you see performing on street corners, pushing against invisible panes of glass. To put it bluntly, he had a complete breakdown. When he started to speak again, he spoke only German. Quoted Freud left and right. Was sent away to a loony bin. Every once in awhile they let him out and he would sneak back on campus, find an empty classroom, and try to misdirect students inside where he would deliver his thoughts on comedy. One theory was that Whitestone was hoping that his son would turn up and that they would recognize each other. Whether that is true or not, I am not qualified to judge. But in fact, last year he managed to get hold of a student roster and sent out some postcards. This year, however, he just got your name. And you wandered in all innocence. We checked Waxman's class and you weren't there. but some one said they saw you entering this building. Good thing we were able to reach you in time. Now if you will just make an appointment to see Professor Waxman, we shall see that you get into the right course with the right teacher....I hope all this hasn't been too traumatic for you, Mr. Nims.

DAVID NIMS: It is confusing.

DEAN OF THE COLLEGE: Isn't it? Life is so confusing. I wonder why we put up with it with such good humor.

DAVID NIMS: It's a very sad story.

DEAN OF THE COLLEGE: Sad. Yes. But he brought it on himself.

DAVID NIMS: Tragic, almost.

DEAN OF THE COLLEGE: Or comic....I guess it all depends upon how you look at things. I myself view his life as simply pathetic. From the Greek *Penthos,* meaning grief or sorrow, although it is the Irish poet William Butler Yeats who claims that Pathos is the nearest to the tragic that the comedian can come....No, you don't have to take notes on this, Mr. Nims. I am not your teacher.

The dean starts toward the door. Mr. Nims sits back down at his desk and stares blankly at his notebook.

DEAN OF THE COLLEGE (*opening the door*): So many times we don't know whether to laugh or to cry.

The dean exits. David Nims stares at the chalkboard with the words comedy and tragedy on the chalk board. He shakes his head.

LIGHTS OUT.

END OF PLAY.

CARAVAN

For Don and Nancy

We are above the Tropic of Cancer, in the Chababa Outpost, somewhere in the Sahara Desert, not far from the Oasis known as Kufra. On stage are two ragged members of the French Foreign Legion–Avery Hopwood and Hoyle Carmichael, two transplanted misfits from out takes of old beau-geste movies. Both men lie flat on the roof of the stockade. Their feet are bare and their uniforms are in tatters.. They are the last two survivors of the worst massacre in Legion history. Hoyle is busy tightening the bandages on his left leg. Avery, with binoculars, surveys the lone and level sands (to pinch a phrase from Shelley) beyond the stockade. A brightly polished bugle lies near bye. Otherwise the stage is bare. Everything is bathed in a pure white light. Call it heat. Both men are in their late twenties or early thirties, but Hoyle is the captain. Avery is the sergeant. Their bodies are muscular and lean and caked with dry blood. A simple white handkerchief flies as a flag.

HOYLE: Is the caravan in sight?
AVERY: No.
BOYLE: No what?
AVERY: No, sir. There is no caravan in sight, Captain.
HOYLE: Good, Sergeant. We have to keep up discipline until the very end.
AVERY: No caravan is not good. Forgive the double negatives, sir.
HOYLE: I sent the water boy with that message days ago. Bring Food, it said. Bring food.
AVERY(*studies the empty canteen*): And water.
BOYLE: There's water at the oasis, right down there.
AVERY: But it will cost us our lives to crawl there.
BOYLE: It will cost us our lives if we don't get there, Sergeant.
AVERY: Unless they've poisoned the oasis.
HOYLE: Unless they've poisoned the oasis. I wouldn't put it past them.
AVERY: What time is it, sir?
HOYLE: looks at his pocket watch.
BOYLE: Three fifteen.
AVERY: We seem to be out of everything but time and sand.

HOYLE: In this hell hole, Sergeant, time and sand are the same thing. That's the principle that brought the hour glass into being.
AVERY: No food. No water. Our entire squadron wiped out.
HOYLE: No need to get melodramatic.
AVERY: I was merely trying to sum up our position, sir. You know, get a fix on things. See where we stand.
HOYLE: We're not standing. At least I'm not. Just keep your eyes fixed on the desert. Watch for the camel driver bringing us food.
AVERY: Food.
BOYLE: Don't think about it.
AVERY: I didn't enjoy eating my boots.
HOYLE: You think I did?
AVERY: You didn't eat my boots. You ate your own boots.
HOYLE: And a treat it was too.
AVERY: More calories than mine.
HOYLE: Why more calories?
AVERY: They were so much larger.
HOYLE: You should have spoken up, Sergeant.
AVERY: I was too busy chewing.
HOYLE: A rat, foaming at the mouth, would be more of a delicacy than that boot. A cornucopia of rabies would be a feast. Keep a sharp look out for the camel.
AVERY: Why do you think, Captain, they call them ships of the desert?
HOYLE: Why do they call what the ships of the desert?
AVERY: That's what I'm asking you.
HOYLE: What are you asking me?
AVERY: Why people call camels the ships of the desert?
HOYLE: What people?
AVERY: Any people.
HOYLE: It must be the heat.
AVERY: People don't call the heat the ship of the desert.
HOYLE: I never said they did, Sergeant. What I meant to imply is that all this heat is getting to us.
AVERY: What heat?
HOYLE: What heat? What do you call all this?
AVERY: All what?
HOYLE: If this is not heat, what is it?

AVERY: I give up. What is it?
HOYLE: I wasn't asking a riddle, Sergeant. I was merely trying to keep civilized conversation alive the only way I know how by talking to another civilized, or reasonably civilized, even unreasonably civilized, human being.
AVERY: We have nothing left.
HOYLE: We have discipline on our side. We don't run amuck like the enemy. Storming walls, slicing heads from necks.
AVERY: Vultures are circling overhead.
HOYLE: We mustn't give up.
AVERY: We mustn't give up.
HOYLE: Well said, Sergeant.
AVERY: Captain, if we mustn't give up then why are we flying a white flag from the tower?
BOYLE: It's the only flag we've got.
AVERY: It doesn't speak well for our side if the only flag we've got is the flag of surrender.
HOYLE: It doesn't speak well for the other side when we put out the flag of surrender and they don't believe us.
AVERY: No one in the Legion has surrendered before.
BOYLE: Catches them off guard, eh? They cone forward to accept our surrender and we blow their heads off.
AVERY: is that cricket?
HOYLE: No, it's not cricket, Sergeant. It's war. It's war to the end. It's all we've got left. We can't fight by the book, when the enemy doesn't... The enemy never fights by the book. That's how we know they're the enemy.
AVERY: But putting out the flag of surrender is a different story.
BOYLE: Surrendering is not giving up.
AVERY: It doesn't appear to be.
HOYLE: Giving in is not the same as giving up. Besides, what rules were the Arabs following when they outnumbered us 800 to 1? What rules, Sergeant?
AVERY: They have the right to outnumber us, Captain.
BOYLE: That's right. Sticking up for the other side, even if you have to eat your bloody boots to do it.
AVERY: I wasn't sticking up for the other side, Captain. But if I have to die, I wish to die with honor.

BOYLE: You'll die with honor, all right. Even if! have to stick it down your throat....It won't taste as good as a boot.
AVERY: They should be preparing for the next attack.
BOYLE: Hand to hand combat and us with no boots.
AVERY: No boots is not good....What time is it, Captain?
BOYLE: Ten thirty.
AVERY: How can that be?
BOYLE: I really don't wish, in my final moments, to explain the origin of time to you, Sergeant. The relationship of the planets to the beating of our hearts, our still, small, sad pulses in the cosmic swing. The alternation of light and dark, day and night. The waning and waxing of the moon in its lunatic conspiracies. The mythic round of the seasons....
AVERY: But ten minutes ago it was only three fifteen.
BOYLE: Pardon me, Sergeant Avery, but when you asked me for the time, I didn't realize that you had a specific time in mind that you wanted. Next time, just let me know. Put in your order.
AVERY: I didn't have any specific time in mind, Captain.
BOYLE: But the watch does. (*He shakes his watch*). The watch is smarter than both of us.
AVERY: Might I have a look at it, sir? The watch.

HOYLE gives the watch to his Sergeant.

HOYLE: Keep one eye on the watch and the other eye on the caravan.
AVERY: Very good, sir. Pause
AVERY: Sir?
HOYLE: What is it, Sergeant?
AVERY: The watch has stopped.
HOYLE: It stopped five or six days ago.
AVERY: So that's why it can be three fifteen one minute and ten thirty the next.
HOYLE: No wonder... I thought I should go out of the world being free of everything.
AVERY: You should have wound it.
HOYLE: We were fighting 20,000 Arabs at the time.
AVERY: But a watch like this ....
BOYLE: I have neglected everything in my life that is why my only human contact is with my enemies or my subordinates. I admit it,

Sergeant. I was derelict in my duty toward that watch, but my hands were filled at the time. I was, in fact, up to my neck in hands.
AVERY: Up to your neck in hands?
BOYLE: I don't know how to say it any other way, being a spare, practical man, who will leave nothing behind in the world. No great estates, no wealth, no children, no statues in the concourse.
AVERY: You should have been a great Captain of Industry.
HOYLE: I should have been anything but the victim of a senseless massacre.
AVERY: It is enough to make one bitter.
HOYLE: Even victory is enough to make one bitter.
AVERY: Is this watch a family heirloom, Captain?
HOYLE: No, Sergeant, it is not. My family disinherited me when they learned I had run away to join the Legion.
AVERY: To Carmichael Hoyle for his inspired leadership and inspiration. Madame Lavinia and her girls .... Inspired leadership and inspiration. Is that not a bit redundant?
HOYLE: They weren't composing literature, Sergeant. They were merely inscribing the back of a watch. They were carried away by the emotions of the moment. Have you never once been carried away by the emotions of the moment?
AVERY: Of course. Who hasn't been?
HOYLE: Oh the Legion has more than its share of brutes. Men who wouldn't shed a tear if you shoved a sword through their stomachs. Men who never wept at a poem or a play, men who would as soon kill you as look at you.
AVERY: The day I took honors in Latin was a great day.

HOYLE removes a ball of string from his pocket.

HOYLE: I'm sure it was.
AVERY: And many a woman, has broken my heart.
HOYLE (*plays with the string*): I'm certain they have.
AVERY: Ah, but to receive an inscribed watch from Madame Lavinia and her girls that must make you very proud.
HOYLE: It does. A small triumph, but what is life but a series of small triumphs and large defeats.

AVERY holds out the watch to give it back.

HOYLE (*not looking at his sergeant*): No, Sergeant, I want you to have it. Keep it.
AVERY: Keep the watch?
HOYLE: Something to remember me by. A keepsake. A memento of your devotion to duty. Not devotion to duty so much. You're just a survivor.
AVERY: I'm touched. I really am.
HOYLE: Take some of this string to chew on. It will help take your mind off things.
AVERY: String I shall take. But I really can't accept your watch. It means too much to you.
HOYLE: I guess you're right.

HOYLE takes back the watch. He puts it in his coat pocket.

HOYLE: But nothing means that much to me anymore. Besides I doubt if I will need a watch where I am going.
AVERY: Where are you going?
BOYLE: To Paris.
AVERY: You're right. Nobody needs a watch in Paris.
BOYLE: Or in Hell.
AVERY: No one needs a watch there either. But you really should make up your mind, sir. There is a big difference between going to Paris and going to Hell.
BOYLE: I most likely not going anywhere, Sergeant.
AVERY: The Caravan will come and rescue us, sir. In the nick of time.
HOYLE: It was a very short note. It shouldn't have taken them all this time to read it.
AVERY: If the water boy got through.
HOYLE: He got through all right. He was a slippery character from the very first.
AVERY: Kept us waiting all the time. We'd cry out for water and he'd take his time bringing it, the water slouching out of the buckets.
BOYLE: Do you have anyone waiting for you?
AVERY: Where?
BOYLE: Back home. Wherever home is.

AVERY: No. Do you?
HOYLE: No. Nobody.
AVERY: This string is filthy.
BOYLE: Don't eat it then.
AVERY: How did I get myself so isolated? I didn't start out this way. There was a time in my life when I was surrounded by family and friends and girls with golden curls and narrow waists, young ladies whose blue eyes were my life's true oasis.
HOYLE: Quite the ladies' man, eh.
AVERY: Not like you.
HOYLE: I never got along with the ladies that well.
AVERY: The inscription on the watch hints otherwise.
HOYLE: There always is a point where women must be paid attention to outside of the bedroom, and it's then I start neglecting them.
AVERY: Joining the Legion is not conducive to a good love life.
HOYLE: Some of us go whichever way the wind blows.
AVERY: Once you get in, you can't get out.
HOYLE: What are you talking about?
AVERY: The Legion.
HOYLE: I thought you. were talking about sex...

The Captain takes out a cigarette. He carefully cuts it in half. He gives one half to the sergeant and keeps the other half for himself. He searches his pockets for a match.

HOYLE Sex is like anything else. You don't know what you need until you no longer have it .... I don't have a match. Do you have a match?

AVERY searches for a match.

AVERY: No.
HOYLE: Damn. Why don't we have things when we need them? A week ago I was up to my ears in matches. Carry something with you your whole life, a dirty piece of string, a match, an address scribbled on a napkin, and then after carrying it about with you for twenty years, toss it away. Next day, you'll need it.
AVERY: You're unduly pessimistic, Captain.
HOYLE: The Legion, she is not known for sweetness and light.

AVERY: Much sweetness here in the tobacco, much light over our heads. Bloody and unbowed.
HOYLE: You romantics are all alike.
AVERY: Romantic? I am not Romantic, Captain. I am the least likely candidate for the Romantic Training Corps.
BOYLE: Oh no, my friend, not so.
AVERY: Why not so?
HOYLE: Because all Romantics search the Universe for Justice and Fair Play.
AVERY: I thought every person did that.
BOYLE: Not all of us. As soon as you start to expect something from life, you romanticize existence.
AVERY: I should live like you? Without expectations?
BOYLE: Live like me. Live like the beasts of the fields. Live any way you choose. Just don't fool yourself.
AVERY: Ah, but you expect the Caravan to reach us in time, bringing us food and water.
BOYLE: I would like it, but I don't expect it. In fact, if the caravan does reach us, I am willing to bet my boots that it will be three hours too late.
AVERY: You no longer have any boots to bet. Neither do I.
BOYLE: I mean the boots we shall buy, if and when we get out of this hell hole. We shall go away on a two week furlough and spend a year's wages.
AVERY: And where shall we go?
BOYLE: Paris. I know a woman in Paris. A remarkable woman. An astronomer. She had hopes of discovering a new star, a new planet, an uncharted galaxy. Whatever she discovered she was going to name after me.
AVERY: The planet Carmichael. Mind boggling to say the least.
BOYLE: To say the least.
AVERY: And did she?
BOYLE: shrugs I don't know. We fell out of love before we got to the discoveries.
AVERY: I have always felt it is the discoveries that cause the falling out of love.

BOYLE: Yes. Well. you are more experienced in those matters than I am. I have always been a painfully shy man. That's why I upped and joined the Legion....It certainly got me out of my father's business.
AVERY: We might as well have been born upon some crater of the moon to end up here like this.
HOYLE: Like how?
AVERY: Like this...Like this...Like this.
HOYLE: It's the heat.
AVERY: It's not the heat.
HOYLE: It's the sand.
AVERY: It's not the sand. It's the growing old and growing away from everything, the twinkling stars of idealism.
HOYLE: It's an illusion. The stars twinkling is an illusion. The moving layers of atmosphere make it seem that the stars are shifting in brightness.
AVERY: What a comfort you are in my time of need.
HOYLE: Don't forget, it's my time of need, too.

AVERY scrambles to the top of a battlement and cries out for the caravan.

AVERY: Caravan!... Caravan!
HOYLE: Good God, man. Get down! Do you want the enemy to know how desperate we are?
AVERY: If they don't know that by now they are too stupid
even to do battle with .... (*shouts across the desert*) Caravan!

AVERY jumps down and picks up the bugle.

AVERY: I'll play the bugle.
HOYLE: You don't know how.
AVERY: I have plenty of time to learn. I'll sound the charge until God in his heaven sits up and takes notice .... Caravan!
HOYLE: Crying for the Caravan is not going to help. All you hear back is an echo of your own desperation.
AVERY: Desperation for what?
BOYLE: To be recognized.

Enter Oort Abdul, the camel driver. He carries with him a large sack that he dumps to the floor.

CAMEL DRIVER: Ah, did someone shout for me?

AVERY turns to face the intruder.

AVERY: Captain, look out!

The Captain reaches for his sword.

BOYLE: Back, dog!
CAMEL DRIVER: Why this greeting? Did you not send for a caravan?
AVERY: The caravan?
HOYLE: You mean the water boy got through?
CAMEL DRIVER: Yes, he did. Allah be praised. Ah, but we had to amputate his arm. Fortunately he had another.

HOYLE and AVERY cross to the sack and untie it.

BOYLE: Food...Food...You don't know how hungry we are.
AVERY: We haven't eaten in days, not counting our boots, of course.
OORT ABDUL: Permit me to introduce myself. I am your humble servant, OOrt Abdul, leader of the Caravan...You are Captain Carmichael Boyle?

HOYLE grunts an answer.

AVERY: That's Captain Boyle Carmichael, and I am Sergeant Avery Bopwood. We are the only two survivors of the massacres at Kufra.
OORT ABDUL: Allah be praised.

During the above, HOYLE and AVERY have been going through the sack of salvation. It is loaded with books. Books and more books. No food. Only books in all languages, sizes and bindings, some in expensive Moroccan bindings.

BOYLE: Allah be praised.

OORT ABDUL: I am honored to be able to bring relief to such distinguished Officers of the Legion.
BOYLE: Relief.
AVERY: Food?... Where's the food?
BOYLE: Where's the bloody food?
AVERY: Food...
OORT ABDUL: Food? What food?
BOYLE: What food? What do you think I sent for? Risked the water boy's life?
OORT ABDUL: But you asked for books.
HOYLE: Books? I'm dying. I don't have time to read.
OORT ABDUL: I am dying too, Captain, but I have time to
bring you books. Good books.The cream of The Library at Alexandria. The Librarian there say, Nothing too good for men of the Legion. Not discards. Not a discard among them.
HOYLE: I asked for food.
OORT ABDUL: I have your note right here.

He produces the note from his sleeve.

OORT ABDUL: See, Captain. It says quite plainly in English. *BOOKS.*
HOYLE: That's not a B. That's an F. That's not a K, that's a D. The little flourish at the end is merely a little curly cue, not an S.
OORT ABDUL: You are quite mistaken.
HOYLE: I wrote that note myself!
OORT ABDUL: Sometimes writers write things that they themselves do not understand.
HOYLE: I was in the heat of battle. I was up to my neck in arms. I scrawled out food on that rag and gave it to the water boy.
OORT ABDUL: You thought food, but you wrote books.

HOYLE takes up his sword I am going to run you through. The caravan leader bares his throat.

OORT ABDUL: Do as you wish. I am your faithful servant.
AVERY: Captain, killing him won't get us anywhere.
HOYLE: I'm in charge here, Sergeant. No matter how extenuating the circumstances.

AVERY: I know that, Captain.
HOYLE: Besides, there is nowhere to get to. This man is obviously one of the enemy, a cousin of Abd-Imam-Muhammad-el-Krim. He deliberately brought us this sack of books to mock our final moments on this earth, taunts us with this sack of learning, turning our heroism into farce.

AVERY has taken the note from the camel driver and is studying it.

AVERY: This word could easily be mistaken for books.
HOYLE: That's right, Sergeant. Take this man's side against me. Take the enemy's side. Go with Abd-Imam-Muhammad-el- Krim. You have joined the wrong side in this Holy War.
AVERY: Sir, ask him about the Caravan. Ask him where are the others. Are they all bringing us books?
OORT ABDUL: Thirty camels at least. All carrying books for you. The rich store of learning throughout the ages. But the Caravan was wiped out. Abd-Imam–Muhammad–el-Krim's men descended on us about three miles from the Oasis.
BOYLE: You mean the Oasis down there?
OORT ABDUL: There is no Oasis down there.
HOYLE: Liar!

The Captain grabs the caravan leader and leads him to the battlement.

HOYLE: You camel driver, what is that blue lagoon down there surrounded by palm trees.
OORT ABDUL: A mirage.
BOYLE: And I suppose I'm a mirage and my Sergeant is a mirage and these infernal books are a mirage. Everything exists in my head, including my wounds.
AVERY: But where are the other members of the caravan? I don't see any other camels.
HOYLE: He's a mirage, Sergeant. A mirage! Get it through your thick skull.
OORT ABDUL: Captain, all my followers were wiped out. From here to Marakesh, the sands are bright red.
AVERY: With blood?

OORT ABDUL: With shame.

AVERY: But you reached us.

OORT ABDUL: The mercy of Allah is infinite.

BOYLE: What is this leading to, Sergeant?

AVERY: Where is his camel? We can kill his camel and eat it.

OORT ABDUL: Ah yes, my camel.

AVERY: You see, Captain, there is still hope.

OORT ABDUL: My camel was slaughtered three days ago. I came by foot, under a broiling sun, carrying on my back what I believed the Captain asked for.

BOYLE: You were sadly mistaken.

OORT ABDUL: Indeed, I was sadly mistaken, but it was my devotion to that mistaken duty, that mirage, if you will, that got me through, that got me this far. I stood on the great and shifting sands, the howling of my Caravan behind me, pitiless moans, and I stared at the tragic blue skies, refusing to give in, knowing that somewhere there was a man, a brave man, a Captain of the Legion, who in his final moments, surrounded by slaughter and horror, cried out for books. How could I deny him?

HOYLE: I wish you had denied me.

OORT ABDUL: Why, Captain? All this desert is a constant reminder of denial.

HOYLE: Better to be constantly denied than to be given the wrong things ....

AVERY: We can eat the books, Captain.

BOYLE: It will come to that. We shall eat our uniforms and our ribbons.

AVERY: There is much nourishment in glue. And the bindings must be from animal skins. Why there is more nourishment on the outside of books than within. We'll divide them equally by pages. Who knows how many calories there are in a page of philosophy?

BOYLE: Philosophy? He had the effrontery to bring me philosophy?

AVERY: Actually, I think of Socrates being thin. Very thin.

OORT ABDUL: The books were all carefully catalogued, Captain.

BOYLE: Yes, you and your cohorts were immensely thoughtful.

OORT ABDUL: But I beg you, Captain...Sergeant...Do not eat the books, sirs....

HOYLE: Look at the camel driver crawl....

OORT ABDUL: On hand and knee and I beg you....Don't eat the books!
AVERY: Why shouldn't we eat the books?
OORT ABDUL: They have all been blessed...Every one of them....They are sacred texts....
HOYLE: The books have been blessed and we haven't been?
OORT ABDUL: I will go back for food...I will run faster than the wind....Yes, it was all my mistake...I see it now. You clearly said food.
AVERY: We can't wait that long. Don't you understand? We're starving.
OORT ABDUL: Then kill me, and devour my flesh. What more can I offer?
BOYLE: You ask me to choose cannibalism over vegetarianism? Are you out of your mind?
OORT ABDUL: You could put it that way if you wish.
HOYLE: Thank you. I'll put it any way I want.
OORT ABDUL: I am sick at heart. All the ideas that man has ever uttered....What kind of men eat books?
HOYLE: I'll utter an idea. The ultimate idea! Die like a dog!

Captain HOYLE rushes at the camel driver with his sword. AVERY grabs the Captain from behind, just in time to prevent the slaying of OORT *ABDUL.*

AVERY: Don't, Captain. You mustn't!
BOYLE: Release me or I'll have you up on charges of mutiny.
AVERY: The Caravan Leader is the only hope we have.
HOYLE: I have to kill him before he spouts any more speeches at me.
AVERY: He'll go back and get us food.
HOYLE: Think Sergeant. Think. If that piece of mirageneous humanity can sneak past Abd-Imam-Muhammad-el-Krim so can we. And that means we can eat that much sooner.
OORT ABDUL: You won't get through, Captain.
BOYLE: Don't overlay my spirit with gelatinous pessimism.
OORT ABDUL: Abd-Imam-Muhammad-el-Krim and his men are just waiting for you to desert your post.. Once you step out of this stockade, this house of learning, as it is now, they will cut you down as quickly as a scythe moves through grain. They will draw blood even from your shadows. But I can get through. They see me as harmless. I will run.

faster than the wind and bring you back food. No more lofty thoughts. I promise. Say the word, and I bring you back food.
HOYLE: Go!
OORT ABDUL: May Allah protect you.

The caravan leader exits, night has fallen upon the scene, but there is a full moon. The two soldiers stand at the battlement and watch the caravan leader disappearing into the night.

BOYLE: I should have killed him.
AVERY: There are so many dead already.

HOYLE lies back down to readjust the bandage upon his wound. The loss of blood has taken its toll upon him.

HOYLE: I don't care what the camel driver says. I'm going to eat the books. I'm going to squeeze every last juice out of those pages.
AVERY: What time is it?
HOYLE: The stars are out. There is a moon. That's your time.

From far out in the desert we hear the sounds of tongues clucking, chanting.

AVERY: Abd-Imam-Muhammad-el-Krim and his men have started their infernal noise-making.
HOYLE: They do not wish us to sleep.
AVERY (*calls from the battlements*): Come and get us, you bastards.
HOYLE: They won't come, Sergeant. They want us to go out there.
AVERY: The sounds seem to be coming closer.
HOYLE: Not very comforting.
AVERY: And cold.
HOYLE: You see all these books, Sergeant? I'll tell you one thing no man ever learns from them.
AVERY: What Captain?
HOYLE: How cold it gets in the desert at night. No matter how hot it has been during the day, no matter how fierce the sun might shine.

The noise-making of Abd-Imam-Muhammad-el-Krim increases.

AVERY: It was hot today, I tell you. I remember it.

HOYLE drifting off Hot...Cold...Paris...What man in his right mind would bring us books?

AVERY: Captain?
HOYLE: Yes, Sergeant?
AVERY: I have been thinking about your offer of the watch:
HOYLE: You have?
AVERY: I was wondering if I could really have it.
HOYLE: Help yourself. It's in the pocket of my jacket.

AVERY takes the watch from the jacket.

AVERY: Thank you, Sir. I shall take good care of it.
HOYLE: I'm sure you will....Read the inscription.
AVERY (to Carmichael): HOYLE for his inspired leadership and inspiration. Madame Lavinia and her girls....
HOYLE: Madame Lavinia and her girls...
AVERY: It keeps just as good time at night as it does at day.
HOYLE: Go on reading, Sergeant.
AVERY: Nothing else inscribed on it...
HOYLE: The books I mean...Just pick out something to read. Read aloud. Let the enemy know we are not like them. That we had the love of something that has a different kind of blood.
AVERY: It's too dark to read, Captain...
HOYLE: Even with the moon?
AVERY: Even with the moon.
HOYLE: I guess you're right, Sergeant....Maybe we should just hold them in our hands for ballast....Yes, let me have that one there, and that one....

AVERY brings the Captain the books and spreads them out over the officer's body. AVERY goes to the battlement and stares out over the sands.

AVERY: I see shapes shifting in the moonlight, Captain.
HOYLE: Romeo, Romeo...Where art thou, Romeo?
AVERY: Thousands and thousands of them coming for us, Captain.

HOYLE: Well, what is it that we have on our side, Sergeant? What kind of books are these?

The sound of the charging enemy is reaching huge proportions.

AVERY: Philosophy, I think he said.
HOYLE: Ah, yes. Philosophy... Well, it is better than nothing, isn't it?
AVERY: I would think so, Sir.
HOYLE: Why in the hell did he bring us books?
AVERY: Shall I recite more from memory?
HOYLE (*feebly*): No..No memory...Shouldn't it have been 'Wherefore thou?'
AVERY: Maybe I could try to read to you.

No response from HOYLE.

AVERY: All these books are in Arabic, Captain.

No response from HOYLE.

AVERY: Maybe there is something here. Maybe I was wrong. Perhaps it is not too dark at all...Captain?

CAPTAIN HOYLE has succumbed to his wounds.

AVERY: It isn't too dark to read by...

AVERY covers HOYLE with the Captain's jacket. The enemy storms the stockade.

LIGHTS OUT.

END OF PLAY.

TERMITES

Lights up on a monk–Brother Peters–holding a censer which he swings slowly back and forth. In the distance, we hear chanting. The chanting fades.

BROTHER PETERS (*directly to the audience*): The guilt of the accused has been clearly proved by the testimony of worthy witnesses and, as it were, by public rumor and inasmuch as the people have humbled themselves before God and supplicated the church to succor them in their distress, it is not fitting to refuse to help and solace them. Walking in the footsteps of the fathers, sitting on the judgment-seat, having the fear of God before our eyes and trusting in his mercy, relying on the counsel of experts, we pronounce and publish our sentence as follows: "In the name and virtue of God, the omnipotent, Father, Son, and Holy Spirit, and of Mary, the most blessed mother of Lord Jesus Christ, and by the authority of the holy apostles Peter and Paul, as well as by that which has made us a functionary in this case, we admonish by these presents the aforesaid locusts and grasshoppers and other animals by whatsoever name they may be called, under pain of malediction and anathema to depart from the vineyards and fields of this district. Within six days from the publication of this sentence and to do no further damage. To do no further damage. If on the expiration of six days, the locusts have refused to obey the injunction, then they are to be anathematized and accursed, and all the animals of the earth are to beseech Almighty God, the dispenser of all good gifts and dispeller of all evils,' to deliver them from so great a calamity."

Lights down. Chanting up. Father Peters exits. Chanting fades. We hear a door slam. Lights up on a large desk, chair, and a coat rack. John Christopher Spires enters. This once distinguished lawyer, now nearing fifty, is dressed in a brown suit and carries a leather briefcase. He removes his coat and hangs it on the rack. Janet Spires, his forty-year-old wife, enters. She carries a tray bearing two martinis.

JANET: How was your day, darling?

CHRISTOPHER (*takes a martini*): Well, to explain my day, I'll need about five of these, thank you.

JANET: Another day without a client? It's been almost two months, hasn't it? It's my fault for making us move so far out into the provinces. But who has ever heard of a town that doesn't need a lawyer?

CHRISTOPHER: Today I've finally landed a client.

JANET: That sounds promising. Who is he? Or she? Do we know them?

CHRISTOPHER: Not he nor she. Try *it*...I am being asked to represent termites.

JANET: Termites? You must be kidding.

CHRISTOPHER: I wish I were. (*An outburst*) I don't want to represent termites!

JANET: Of course not, darling. Who does? Would Clarence Darrow represent a creature that sees a piano as a source of protein?

CHRISTOPHER: I'll be the laughing stock of the legal profession! There goes the termite lawyer. What will be next? Ants? Lice? Soon inanimate objects will demand legal services. The grapefruit divorce acts of 1376.

JANET: Grapefruits are living things.

CHRISTOPHER: Don't get technical with me. We aren't in court.

JANET: I have no idea what you're talking about. You've barely have had one martini and you're raving about termites.

CHRISTOPHER: The Cloister of Our Lady of the Mercies is infested with them. Thousands of termites. Millions for all I know. Being deprived of sex education in school, I don't know how termites breed. But all they seem to do all day is create more termites. The good monks informed me that the queen termite lays some 68,000 eggs a day. Sawdust acts as some kind of aphrodisiac!...Bring me my chainsaw of desire!

JANET: Obviously, the cloister needs an exterminator.

CHRISTOPHER: The cloister has an exterminator.

JANET: Who?

CHRISTOPHER: The Catholic Church. Listen to this, Janet, the monks don't wish to bring bodily harm to the termites, they merely want the termites to abandon the premises. At the same time, the Monks feel strongly that the termites should have the right to present their side of the case, and so the Church is willing to subsidize a lawyer to represent the interests of the termites. After weighing my superior qualifications, the Church feels I am that man...Other lawyers get to defend movie stars. I have clients who eat excrement.

During the above, Janey has exited. Christopher puts on his coat and takes his seat behind his desk. Brother Peters enters.

CHRISTOPHER: Let's see, Brother Peters, I am supposed to go into court and represent the rights of the termites.

BROTHER PETERS: That's correct. You see it wouldn't be right for our side to have ecclesiastical and legal representation and not grant that same right to our opponents. The termites need a lawyer.

CHRISTOPHER: You must forgive me. Not only am I new to this community, I am new to these customs. You have experience in these matters?

BROTHER PETERS: Oh yes. Some years ago, Jean Darat, the eminent lawyer represented a tribe of locusts that were causing a great deal of harm to our crops. He argued brilliantly, but our side had much the stronger case. One had only glance out the window to see he evidence.

CHRISTOPHER: Then I suggest you hire Jean Darat. He has experience in defending insects. I have defended other lawyers. That is close to the insect world as I care to get.

BROTHER PETERS: Well, there are two objections to your suggestion. First, Darat, as I have mentioned, lost his case. The Termites are adverse to be associated with a loser. Second, Darat is dead. The case of our City versus the Locusts is over forty years old. I suggest, however, you study the transcripts. You may find them useful. Of course, termites are not locusts.

CHRISTOPHER: Termites are not locusts. May I quote you on that?

BROTHER PETERS: Being facetious will not improve your standing in our community.

CHRISTOPHER: And if do not take the case?

BROTHER PETERS: It would not be wise to turn a deaf ear to our cause. Every one in this province takes this matter very seriously. You are new here. Persons will be reluctant to hire a lawyer who is anti-church.

CHRISTOPHER: I am not anti-church. I am anti-termite.

BROTHER PETERS: You must not be anti-termite. Termites are like us created by God. Therefore, are loved by God. Therefore are deserving

of God's great gift–Justice. By granting us Justice, God shows His love for us. By allowing the termites their day in court we are reflecting God's love.
CHRISTOPHER: I love living in a community where I am being told what to believe.
BROTHER PETERS: Mr. Spires, correct me if I am wrong, but did we drag you and your wife here against your will?

Lights down. Chants under. Lights up on Christopher at his desk with his head down. His head is surrounded by stacks of ancient law books and emptied vodka bottles and coffee cups. Janet enters carrying more books.

JANET: Have you found anything yet, dear?
CHRISTOPHER (*not lifting his head*): What?
JANET: Maybe you should go to bed...You're working yourself into an early grave.
CHRISTOPHER (*lifts his head, tries to revive himself*): I can't even interview my clients.
JANET: Have you tried?
CHRISTOPHER: Have I tried? What do you mean have I tried? I don't talk termite. I tried to set up several appointments, but termites don't keep appointments. They're blind. They live in utter darkness their entire lives. They never go outside...maybe they would like me better if I had a wooden leg.
JANET: Perhaps it would give you some ideas if you observed the termites at work.
CHRISTOPHER: What am I suppose to do? Drive out to the Cloister and drop in unexpectedly? Why couldn't I have been given locusts to defend or ants? Then I could be out in the sunshine getting a tan. Do you know how depressing it is to have to crawl under a porch to give your client a bill?
JANET: Termites are not locusts.
CHRISTOPHER: You're the second person in three weeks who has told me that. But neither termites nor locusts take you out to lunch...And they can't read. I have to read all the legal notices to them so that they understand what is going on...Of course they can't hear me over all the chewing.
JANET: Try to be more sympathetic to your clients.

CHRISTOPHER: More sympathetic? Look at the legs of my desk. The other night I got down on all fours and tried eating wood just to see what it tastes like. How many lawyers can you name who have splinters on their tongue?
JANET: I hear they all do.
CHRISTOPHER: Very funny. You can be sympathetic to termites but not to your own husband.
JANET: I'm doing the best I can
CHRISTOPHER: So am I.
JANET: And so are the termites, most likely.
CHRISTOPHER: What does that mean?
JANET: In one of the old books in the city hall, I believe I found something useful...
CHRISTOPHER: What?
JANET (*opens a dusty book and points out the appropriate page*): This. On May 8th, 1546, the distinguished lawyer Claude Morel, defending locusts...
CHRISTOPHER: Locusts...Always locusts. How come they can afford all the good lawyers? Do they have pockets?
JANET: Quiet. Listen. Morel said: "In as much as God, the Supreme author of all that exits, hath ordained that the earth should bring forth fruits and herbs (*animas vegetativas*), not solely for the sustenance of rational beings, but likewise for the preservation of support of insects, which fly about on the surface of the soil, therefore it would be unbecoming to proceed with rashness and precipitance against the insects now actively accused and indicted; on the contrary, it would be more fitting for us to have recourse to the mercy of Heaven to implore pardon for our sins."
CHRISTOPHER: Do you think it will go well for me, in an ecclesiastical court, to charge the church with rashness and recipitance? Especially when the Church has been bringing insects and other animals to justice for hundreds of years?
JANET: Try for a change of venue. Why should termites be tried in a ecclesiastical court?
CHRISTOPHER: Because in this instance human life hasn't been lost. If, for example, a pig ate a child, then the pig would be tried in a civil court and, if found guilty, executed in public. Most likely guillotined. Voila! Bacon!...Here, my love, try these on for size.

He hands her a wrapped package.

JANET: What is it?
CHRISTOPHER: A reward for all your hours of research.

She unwraps the package. She holds up two pair of large termite wings, the kind found on the body of the black mound termite.

JANET: Wings? What are these for?
CHRISTOPHER: You'll see. Put them on. Let's see how they look.

Lights down. Enter Brother Peters and Brother Matthias, who will act as the presiding judge of the Ecclesiastical Court. Lights up as Brother Matthias takes his place behind the desk. Brother Peters and Christopher stand in front. Christopher holds a brown paper bag and a thin book on termites–Dwellers in Darkness *by S. H. Skaife.*

BROTHER MATTHIAS (*ringing a bell*): I hereby call the Ecclesiastical Court in session, with the case of The Brothers of the Cloister of Our Lady of Mercy versus the Termites of the same cloister. Who represents the Cloister in this action?
BROTHER PETERS: I do, Brother Matthias. I am Brother Peters of the Cloister in question.
BROTHER MATTHIAS: The Cloister is not in question here, Brother Peters...Now who represents the Termites?
CHRISTOPHER: I do, your honor.
BROTHER MATTHIAS (*taking notes with a quill pen on parchment*): And you are?
CHRISTOPHER: John Christopher Spires of the Province of Aix.
BROTHER MATTHIAS: And where are your clients, Mr. Spires?
CHRISTOPHER: My clients?
BROTHER MATTHIAS: Yes, usually when a person, animal, or insect is charged with a crime, it is a requirement that the accused be present in court. Is that not so?
CHRISTOPHER: Yes, your honor. But you must admit that this a highly unorthodox case.
BROTHER MATTHIAS: No, I don't have to admit that. I am not here to admit anything but evidence. And I shall not have evidence

presented against the accused unless the accused is present in the courtroom. The Church has held these trials before you know, so the idea of bringing insects to court is not as unusual as you would have the court believe. When the eminent lawyer Claude Morel defended locusts his clients were present in the court room.

CHRISTOPHER: Yes, but termites are not locusts.

BROTHER MATTHIAS: That is very astute...I must write that down. Termites are not locusts.

Lights down. Sound of rain. Then, lights up. Brother Peters enters; then Janet, carrying an umbrella and the large, nearly invisible termite wings.

JANET: Brother Peters, you must help me!

BROTHER PETERS: I am here only to serve. How may I be of service?

JANET: It's my husband. You must take him off the case.

BROTHER PETERS: I'm afraid that's not in my power. Once a lawyer has been retained, only the termites can decide whether they wish to continue with their lawyer.

JANET: But the case is driving my husband to insanity. He's becomes obsessed.

BROTHER PETERS: I know he has been putting a lot of time and effort into this case. It is building his standing in our community. Once the outcome is decided, both you and he will reap the benefits.

JANET: It's destroying our marriage.

BROTHER PETERS: I was under the impression that it was bringing you closer together, that you were helping your husband prepare the defense.

JANET (*holds forth the giant termite wings*): You see these?

BROTHER PETERS: What are they?

JANET: Termite wings. He first started chewing the legs off our furniture. Now he's moved on to these.

BROTHER PETERS (*studying the giant wings*): Termite wings?

JANET: What kind of a man gives his wife giant replicas of termite wings?

BROTHER PETERS: You have to be patient with me. My knowledge of marriage is extremely limited. Only what I pick up between the lines of the *Song of Solomon.*

JANET: My husband expects me to run outside naked, wearing only these wings. Then he chases me until the wings fall off. It's the dropping of the wings that turns him on. He wants us to make love at eleven in the morning in the branches of a tree. You can imagine its impact upon our neighbors. They have small children to consider...The telephone repairmen in our neighborhood haven't moved in two weeks...I'm sorry, Brother Peters, you're blushing.
BROTHER PETERS: I'm basically a shy man. I blush reading *The Song of Solomon.* I don't really understand that part of the woman's lover feeding among the lilies.
JANET: Feeding among the lilies is much more pleasant than frolicking naked in a pine tree during the rainy season. Both my husband and I are coming down with colds.
BROTHER PETERS: Your husband is certainly doing a disservice to his clients.
JANET: That's what I think. That's why I think the Church should recruit another lawyer.
BROTHER PETERS: No, you misunderstand me. I was referring to the fact that termites don't mate in trees. The mate in the soil, in holes in the earth.
JANET: Ah!
BROTHER PETERS: Why Ah?
JANET: My husband has been digging a tunnel under the house.
BROTHER PETERS: The female digs a small chamber about two inches or so below the surface… It's about a half an inch in diameter, and a male and female termite crawl inside, they close up the tunnel, and there they stay throughout the winter. It is very likely that copulation doesn't take place until the spring, when warmer weather arrives.
JANET: And you say you don't know much about married life.
BROTHER PETERS: Well, I have done my homework. I have to know who my opponents are. I trust your husband is merely doing the same.

Lights down. Lights up on Brother Peters.

BROTHER PETERS: Your husband is certainly doing a disservice to his clients.
JANET: That's why I think the Church should recruit another lawyer.

BROTHER PETERS: No, you misunderstand me. I was referring to the fact that termites don't mate in trees. They mate in the soil, in holes in the earth.
JANET: Ah!
BROTHER PETERS: Why Ah?
JANET: My husband has been digging a tunnel under the house.
BROTHER PETERS: The female digs a small chamber about two inches or so below the surface... It's about a half an inch in diameter, and a male and female termite crawl inside, they close up the tunnel, and there they stay throughout the winter. It is very likely that copulation doesn't take place until the spring, when warmer weather arrives.
JANET: And you say you don't know much about married life.
BROTHER PETERS: Well, I have done my homework. I have to know who my opponents are. I trust your husband is merely doing the same.

Lights down. Lights up on Christopher at his desk. Burning the midnight oil. Janet appears at the door.

JANET: Aren't you coming to bed? It's very late.
CHRISTOPHER: I'm chewing over *The Life of the White Ant* by Maeterlinck, white ant being another name for termite.
JANET: And what does Maeterlinck have to say.
CHRISTOPHER (*takes up a sheet of paper*): "Here we have obviously an absolute communism, a communism of the esophagus and the bowels, a collective cacoprophagy. In this flourishing republic no loss is permitted of anything that, from the economic point of view...If a termite happens to change its sin, the slough is immediately devoured. Should one die worker, king, queen, or warrior the corpse is forthwith eaten by the survivors."
JANET: I am sure that is very fascinating dear, but I am going to bed and I think you should too. Aren't you due in court by 10 A.M?

Janet exits.

CHRISTOPHER (*still reading*): "There is no waste. The clearance is automatic and always profitable: everything is good, nothing lies about, everything is edible, everything is cellulose, and the excrement is used almost indefinitely over and over again."

He pauses for a moment, studies the paper in his hand, then crumples it, tears off pieces and starts to eat them.

CHRISTOPHER: God, does Maeterlinck taste good. Much better tasting than that Shakespearean quarto I nibbled upon at lunch. Maybe I had better wash it down with a few wood shavings from the leg of my desk.

CHRISTOPHER gets down on all fours and starts to gnaw at the leg of his desk.

CHRISTOPHER: Everything is cellulose....Of course, Janet isn't entirely cellulose, is she?

Lights down. Then up. Enter Brother Peters and Brother Matthias, the presiding judge of the Esslesiastical Court. Lights up as Brother Matthias takes his place behind the desk. Brother Peters and Christopher stand in front. Christopher holds a paper bag.

BROTHER MATTHIAS: Have you managed to convince your clients to attend their own trial?
CHRISTOPHER: Well, I am certain you would not want your courtroom furniture over run with termites, your honor, and so I brought a representative sample in this bag.
BROTHER MATTHIAS: May I see?
CHRISTOPHER: Yes, your honor.

He gives the paper bag to Brother Matthias who proceeds to empty out its contents on his desk.

BROTHER MATTHIAS: They aren't moving?
CHRISTOPHER: No, your honor.
BROTHER MATTHIAS (*pokes the insects with a pencil*): They appear to be dead.
CHRISTOPHER: They are dead.

BROTHER MATTHIAS sweeps the termites into a waste paper basket.

BROTHER MATTHIAS: Well, so much for appearances...Is this your way of insulting our court, dragging dead bodies before us?

CHRISTOPHER: No, your honor. My clients weren't dead when we first discussed meeting here. But the exposure to the dry air of our region has not been to their benefit. Termites need humid air in which to exist, air saturated with a high nitrogen content. Fresh air is a termite's enemy. Thus, I am trying to demonstrate to this court why it is impossible for my clients to be present at this trial. Even if the termites could survive outside their terminary, they would be subject to all sorts of attacks from their enemies. Certainly the court would not want to endanger the life of one God's creatures.

BROTHER PETERS: I object.

BROTHER MATTHIAS: On what grounds?

BROTHER PETERS: My worthy opponent is trying to win sympathy for his client by parading their corpses before us.

CHRISTOPHER: It's not exactly a parade, even by the most loose of definitions.

BROTHER MATTHIAS: Objection denied. I find it difficult to conceive how much sympathy can come into play for a dead termite.

CHRISTOPHER: Seventeen dead termites, to be precise.

BROTHER MATTHIAS: Very well. Seventeen dead termites.

CHRISTOPHER: I know that in previous trials, ants have been paraded into the courtroom. Locusts, too, I imagine. But termites and daylight don't mix. I hope that since this is an ecclesiastical court that the court will believe that I am representing my clients in good faith.

BROTHER MATTHIAS: It's not your faith we doubt. It is the need for the client to be aware of what is happening in this court. The Termites must be represented in some form just in case their own lawyer introduces evidence that they might not want to be introduced.

CHRISTOPHER: I have anticipated that problem, your honor. I have an ant in my briefcase. The ant shall act as a silent witness to what goes on here and shall report back to the termites.

BROTHER MATTHIAS: If Brother Peters agrees.

CHRISTOPHE: There is precedent. As you are no doubt aware, Old German law allowed dogs, cats, and roosters to act as witnesses say, in cases of burglary, where there had been no other witnesses.

BROTHER PETERS: I have no objection. Does this go-between of yours have a name?

CHRISTOPHER: Ethelred.
BROTHER MATTHIAS: Is Ethelred ready?

Christopher opens his briefcase and peers inside.

CHRISTOPHER: Ethelred is ready.
BROTHER MATTHIAS: Proceed, Brother Peters. Make your case against the Termites.
CHRISTOPHER: Excuse me, your honor. There is one other legal point that should be addressed before the trial commences.
BROTHER MATTHIAS (*pouring a glass of water from a pitcher of water)*: And what is that?
CHRISTOPHER: Whether the accused should be tried as laity or clergy.
BROTHER MATTHIAS: Termites have not taken holy orders. Therefore, how shall we regard them as priests?
CHRISTOPHER: They have eaten holy wood. Devoured scripture, I imagine.
BROTHER PETERS: Is the esteemed John Christopher Spires, Esquire confusing Termites with Bookworms?
CHRISTOPHER: I am not. But my clients, the Termites of the Cloister of Our Lady of Mercies, have been accused to devouring a substantial part of the Cross of Christ. Certainly that makes them holy.
BROTHER MATTHIAS: All of God's creation is holy. That is a given. But eating god is not the same as obeying him. In fact, it is a tactless thing to do. Therefore, in this court, the Termites of the Cloister of Our Lady of Mercies shall be tried as laity .... There is precedent for my judgment too, Mr. Spires.
CHRISTOPHER: I accept your decision without exception.
BROTHER MATTHIAS: Thank you. Now Brother Peters proceed.

Brother Peters holds up a wooden chair that is filled with tiny holes and whose legs have been partially eaten away.

BROTHER PETERS: I should have this marked Exhibit A.
BROTHER MATTHIAS: Is that a tennis racquet?
BROTHER PETERS: It's a chair, your honor... Or what's left of it.

Lights down. Chants up. Christopher sits at his desk. There is a small pile of sawdust near his left elbow. Seated on a chair next to the desk is a giant black ant. It crosses one pair of legs. Christopher snacks on the sawdust while he studies a few pages of legal document.

CHRISTOPHER: I understand your point of view.
ANT: Chryxxx mere mia mia moaner.
CHRISTOPHER: It's so refreshing to speak with a creature I can understand. Over the past few weeks my wife was completely incomprehensible.
ANT: Chryxxx mere mia mia moaner.
CHRISTOPHER: No need to repeat yourself. My computer program translates quickly.
ANT: Quasmare.
CHRISTOPHER: Is there an umlaut over *quasmare*?

The giant ant shakes his head.

CHRISTOPHER: Point well taken.
ANT: I'll speak English if you prefer. God knows I've spent enough hours crawling over Webster's Unabridged .... When I was much smaller, of course.
CHRISTOPHER: I think it's very obvious what Atomic testing has done to your species. Before you belonged to the natural world, you and your kind knew your place in nature. But now you're only fit to star in Hollywood movies. Horror films at that. That is about as low as a living creature can fall.
ANT (*dramatically*): To be a pismire or not to be a pismire. That is the all purpose philosophic conundrum.
CHRISTOPHER: I believe you have a strong case against all those governments that have indulged in atomic testing. Unfortunately, I am tied up in a very complicated case involving termites.

The giant ant makes a giant gagging sound.

CHRISTOPHER: Exactly. That's how I feel about termites too, but I was coerced into representing them. Thus, I am not in position to give your case the attention it deserves. At least not right at the moment.

The giant ant stands up, picks up a burlap sakc, and dumps a huge pile of paer money on the lawyer's desk.

CHRISTOPHER: Where do ants get so much money?
ANTS: We have a strong union and we work hard. There's not a movie made in Hollywood that doesn't have at least one ant in it.
CHRISTOPHER: I have a feeling that the Termite case will be resolved shortly. If you would be willing to wait two or three weeks, I shall be glad to accept a modest retainer...How much money is here, do you think.
ANT: Three billion, two hundred million, and five dollars.
CHRISTOPHER: Fair enough. Why not see me two weeks from today, and we'll get started suing the government for all it's worth. We'll show the nations of the world they can't create mutations willy nilly.
ANT: We once were Democrats. Now look at us.

Lights out. Gregorian chant under. Lights up. Brother Peters with Brother Matthias. They are tapping into a keg of wine. Brother Peters carries a badminton racket (or is it a small chair?)

BROTHER PETERS: Do you sense something strange going on?
BROTHER MATTHIAS: Everything seems quite normal to me. God is in His Heaven and all's moderate with the world.
BROTHER PETERS: No doubt.
BROTHER MATTHIAS: No doubt makes for a much better world.
BROTHER PETERS: Well, I have doubts.
BROTHER MATTHIAS: About?
BROTHER PETERS: About two weeks ago.
BROTHER MATTHIAS: Not exactly what I meant.
BROTHER PETERS: About two weeks ago, Mr. Spires' wife came to me and asked for help with certain marital problems.
BROTHER MATTHIAS: That's not unusual. Even I cannot but help notice their marriage undergoing unusual strains. Overwork on Mr. Spires part. Defending termites is the most demanding case a lawyer can undertake. That's why questions about it are frequently omitted from the Bar Exam.
BROTHER PETERS: But I haven't seen Mrs. Spires since then.

BROTHER MATTHIAS: Perhaps she has gone away. A brief vacation from her overworked husband. A visit to her family. A sick relative.
BROTHER PETERS: No. No one has seen her. No one has seen Mrs. Spires leave the town. No one has seen her leave her house. I called several times when I knew Mr. Spires would not be home and there was never an answer.
BROTHER MATTHIAS: Didn't the Pope warn us about watching Rear Window We must not pry into the private lives of our citizens. If our parishioners come to us. That's one thing.
BROTHER PETERS: Mrs. Spires can't come to us. I'm certain of it. Do you notice that when he speaks of Mrs. Spires, he uses the past tense?
BROTHER MATTHIAS: You suspect foul play?
BROTHER PETERS: I believe he ate her.
BROTHER MATTHIAS: Ate her? My God, man! Do you know what you're saying?
BROTHER PETERS: Of course I know what I'm saying. I'm not some insect babbling indecipherable signals.
BROTHER MATTHIAS: I've been informed ants speak good English.
BROTHER PETERS: That's because there are so many of them. A few, I suppose, can place a noun with a verb, which is more most high school students can do these days.
BROTHER MATTHIAS: You have proof?
BROTHER PETERS: Of course, I have proof. Any fool can go about claiming a man has destroyed his wife. And he'd be correct nine times out of ten, but it takes a man of rare precision who can produce the requisite evidence...You agree that Mr. Spires has been acting most unstable.
BROTHER MATTHIAS: I agree. But I attributed to the fact " the behaviour of the *Kalotermitidae* during the period of swarming and colony foundation is very unstable." At least that was Luscher's observation.
BROTHER PETERS: And you saw our friend the other day in the courtroom when he picked up a hymnal and devoured it for lunch.
BROTHER MATTHIAS: It was a Protestant hymnal. I didn't mind.
BROTHER PETERS: While Mr. Spires was eating the Protestant hymnal, I left the courtroom, snuck back to his house, opened a window and entered. I went down to the basement, opened the furnace. (*from under his robe, he produces a large human bone*) Behold! The

remains of Janice Spires .... It's a little ragged because on the way to the lab for DNA testing, one of our Saint Bernards saw it and took a liking to it.

BROTHER MATTHIAS: Quite a tug of war, I imagine.

BROTHER PETERS: I won. And the DNA definitely proves that it belongs to Janet Spires.

BROTHER MATTHIAS: But he burned her? He didn't eat her?

BROTHER PETERS: No. Like a termite, he devoured her. But there was the problem of leftovers. He burned the bones. You know how some Lawyers feel about evidence. It merely gets in the way of their arguments. ..But this one bone will bring our friend to justice.

BROTHER MATTHIAS: Justice.

BROTHER PETERS: Or as much Justice as it is possible for humans to create.

BROTHERS MATTHIAS: Don't you feel responsible?

BROTHER PETERS: In what way?

BROTHER MATTHIAS: Well, we did coerce him to take on the case of the termites.

BROTHER PETERS: We asked him to defend the termites. We did not ask him to become one. Free Will, Brother Matthias. There is no substitute for Free Will.

Lights down. Music up. The Beach Boys, perhaps. Lights up on Chrisopher Spires. Christopher is standing on top of his desk. He wears the giant termite wings and his neck is in a noose. The rope disappears up away above him. Pacing back and forth on the desktop, he reads from a court document.

CHRISTOPHER: Those irrational and imperfect creations, the termite and the ant, called imperfect because there were none of those species on Noah's Ark and at the time of the great deluge. But after the Flood, the ants and the termites rose up "in numerous bands and have done immense damage to the ground and above the ground to the perceptible diminution of food for man and animal; and to the end that such things may cease, my gracious Lord has commanded in his name to admonish the aforesaid termites and ants to withdraw from our precincts and to abstain from further destruction of property. Therefore, by the command of Jesus Christ and in His name and also by virtue of the high and holy Trinity, and through the merits of the redeemer of Mankind, our Saviour Jesus Christ, and in virtue and dedication to the Holy Church, I do command and admonish you, each and all, every crawling thing to depart within the next six days from all places where you and have secretly and greatly done or might still do damage, also to depart from all fields, meadows, gardens, pastures, trees, hills, and all spots where things nutritive to man and to beast spring up and grow."

The giant ant bearing handcuffs and a warrant for the arrest of the lawyer enters. Christopher pays no attention.

CHRISTOPHER: "If you do not heed this admonition or obey these commands, and think you have some reason not to comply with them, I admonish, notify, and summon you in virtue and Obedience to the Holy Church to appear on the sixth day after this execution at precisely one o'clock after midday at Wifflisburg, there to justify yourselves and to answer for your conduct."

ANT: You talking to me?

CHRISTOPHER: What are you doing here?

ANT: I have come to arrest you for the foul murder and cannibalization of your wife Janet Spires.

CHRISTOPHER: The Sheriff is using giant ants as his deputies?

ANT: It's ironic, isn't it? One moment I was on side of the law and today I am on the other. It just goes to show you that in Law, as in sex, size matters.

CHRISTOPHER: You're not taking me alive. You see this rope about my neck? I'll hang myself before I ever stand trial.

ANT: Why not stand trial? You might be found not guilty.

CHRISTOPHER: No. I am guilty. I am guilty as Hell. I took my beloved wife in my arms and in a moment of frenzy I devoured her.

ANT: How did she taste?

CHRISTOPHER: How did she taste? What kind of unfeeling, unsympathetic, insensitive response is that?

ANT: I'm only an ant. My goal in life is to ruin as many picnics as possible.

CHRISTOPHER: What I am suffering is no picnic. Believe me.

ANT: I know nothing about sympathy. I do as I am programmed. All I can tell you is that from an ant's perspective Free Will is over rated.

CHRISTOPHER: Well., then I can tell you that human flesh as a delicacy is over-rated. I prefer a good furniture leg. Cellulose is the key to mankind's survival.
ANT: Christopher Spires, I command you to come down and come with me in the name of the law?
CHRISTOPHER: Law? Here my answer....God, forgive me!

He leaps from the desk but the rope breaks. He falls in a heap. The giant ant quickly approaches him and helps the shaken lawyer to his feet.

CHRISTOPHER: What happened?
ANT: I believe some insects gnawed their way through the hemp. That's the way it looks to me...*(displays the frayed end of rope)* See the teeth marks?
CHRISTOPHER: Damn those termites! Why did God ever create insects in the first place?
ANT: I'm afraid we insects see things differently. Come along, Mr. Spires. I'm afraid you won't be handling my lawsuit against the government.

LIGHTS OUT.

END OF PLAY.

Note: for the opening and closing longer speeches of "Termites", I am indebted to *The Criminal Prosecution and Capital Punishment of Animals* by E.P. Evans (1906).

ACKNOWLEDGEMENTS

The Death of the Siamese Twins was originally published in *CrazyQuilt*, Vol. 2 (March, 1987). The play was originally produced at the WPA Theatre. It was directed by John Schak. The actors were: Janice Fuller, Gina McMather, and Charlie Stavola.

Night Fishing in Antibes was originally produced at the Philipstown Depot Theatre as part of its 8th One Act Play Festival. The production was directed by Giom Grech.

Foils was originally published in *The Molicha Review*. *Foils* was originally produced at the Philipstown Depot Theatre as part of its 7th One Act Play Festival. The actors were: Kara Greevy, Lan Grullo, Margaret Norton, Jay Reiner, and Lucy Knisley. The play was directed by Eileen Charbonneau.

Tragedy: a Comedy was originally published in *The Georgia Review* (Fall, 2000).

Caravan was originally published in WEST, No. seven (summer, 1992). It was produced at the Apple Corps Theater, under the direction of John Kennedy.

PRODUCTION RECORD

A BRIEF SELECTION OF PUBLISHED WORKS:

The Envoi Messages (published by Broadway Play Publishers)
Plays (A collection of comic one-acts, published by Broadway Play Publishers)
Warbeck (George Spelvin's Theater Journal)
Arbuckle's Rape (Prologue Press)
The Last of the Marx Brothers' Writers (West Coast Plays #2)
God Have Mercy on the June Bug (Modern International Drama)
Goin' West (Best Short Plays, 1977)
The Ballroom in St. Patrick's Cathedral (Aran Press)
The Singer in the White Pajamas (Dramatic Publishing Co.)
Crazy Juke (Chicago Review)
Tragedy: A Comedy (The Georgia Review)
The Singer in the White Pajamas (The Georgia Review)
The Mind-Readers (Massachusetts Review)
16 Points on a Hurricane's Compass (Aran Press)
Making It Up as We Go Along (one-acts about Theater, Aran Press)

PRODUCTIONS (BRIEF SELECTION OF FULL-LENGTH PLAYS):

The Envoi Messages–Indiana Repertory Theater ; Willows Theatre Co (Concord, CA).
The Last of the Marx Brothers' Writers–Brandeis University; Old Globe; Cleveland Playhouse; Solari Theater (Beverly Hills).
The Ballroom in St. Patrick's Cathedral–Colonnades Theatre Lab (NYC).
Warbeck–Colonnades Theatre Lab (NYC).
The Great American Quiz Show Scandal–University of Southern California at San Diego.
Arbuckle's Rape–Theatre Rappaport (Los Angeles); Westbeth (NYC).
Alchemy Da Vinci–State University of New York at Binghamton.
The Collaborators–Stetson University (DeLand, Florida).

LOUIS PHILLIPS

He is a widely published poet, playwright, and short story writer. He has written some 35 books for children and adults. Among his works are: A DREAM OF COUNTRIES WHERE NO ONE DARE LIVE (SMU Press) and THE BUS TO THE MOON (Fort Schuyler Press), short story collections; HOT CORNER, a collection of his baseball writings from Livingston Press; THE ENVOI MESSAGES, a full-length play (Broadway Play Publishers); PLAYS: A COLLECTION OF COMIC ONE-ACTS (Broadway Play Publishers); 16 POINTS ON A HURRICANE'S COMPASS (Aran Press); and, THE AUDIENCE BOOK OF THEATRE QUOTATIONS (World Audience Publishers). He lives in Manhattan with his wife Pat Ranard, and their two sons Ian and Matthew.

The Audience
Book of
Theatre Quotations
by Louis Phillips

Printed in the United States
82522LV00006B/196-198

9 781934 209301